Contents

D1229443

Units	Competencies	Workforce Skills
Communication	Communicate information Acquire and interpret information	Understand a simple form Ask for and give personal information Introduce oneself Complete a simple form
Your Workplace	Acquire and evaluate information Understand organizational systems Interpret and communicate information	Identify places at work Ask for and give directions Ask for and find common supplies
Technology	Select technology Apply technology to specific tasks Teach others	Identify common machines Give and follow instructions to use a machine Read simple instructions
Time Management	Allocate time Organize and maintain information	Say the time, date, and day of the week Ask for and give personal information Complete a simple form
Customer Service	Serve clients/customers Monitor and correct performance Understand organizational systems Interpret and communicate information	Recognize good customer service Greet customers Take customer orders Offer assistance to customers Apologize and correct errors
Culture of Work	Understand social and organizational systems Participate as a member of a team Allocate time Acquire and evaluate information	Report lateness or absence Understand company rules Understand good work habits Use public transportation to get to work
Finances	Interpret and communicate information Serve clients and customers Acquire and evaluate information	Understand amounts of money Count money and make change Write a check Cash one's paycheck Make a deposit
Health and Safety	Acquire and evaluate information Understand technological systems Interpret and communicate information	Identify parts of the body State symptoms and injuries Read safety signs Call 911 Identify unsafe working conditions Follow safety instructions
Working with People	Recognize teamwork skills Participate as a member of a team Work with people from culturally diverse backgrounds Interpret/communicate information Allocate time Monitor and correct performance	Introduce oneself Greet coworkers Get along with coworkers Accept feedback Correct an error Understand company rules
Career Development	Acquire and evaluate information Interpret and communicate information Allocate time Negotiate	Identify kinds of jobs Give one's work experience Read help-wanted ads and signs Complete a simple job application

Each unit of *English ASAP* systematically presents one or more SCANS Competencies.
The SCANS Foundation Skills are integrated throughout the instruction.

Steck-Vaughn

English ASAP™

Connecting English to the Workplace

SCANS Consultant

Andrea Perrault
Connected Resources—Learning that Works!
Boston, Massachusetts

Program Consultants

Judith Dean-Griffin
ESL Teacher
Windham Independent School District
Texas Department of Criminal Justice
Huntsville, Texas

Marilyn K. Spence
Workforce Education Coordinator
Orange Technical Education Centers
Mid-Florida Tech
Orlando, Florida

Brigitte Marshall
English Language Training
for Employment Participation
Albany, California

Dennis Terdy
Director, Community Education
Township High School District 214
Arlington Heights, Illinois

Christine Kay Williams
ESL Specialist
Towson University
Baltimore, Maryland

STECK-VAUGHN
C O M P A N Y

A Division of Harcourt Brace & Company

Acknowledgments

Executive Editor:	Ellen Northcutt
Supervising Editor:	Tim Collins
Assistant Art Director:	Richard Balsam
Interior Design:	Richard Balsam, Jill Klinger
Electronic Production:	Jill Klinger, Stephanie Stewart, Alan Klemp, David Hanshaw
Assets Manager:	Margie Foster

Editorial Development: Course Crafters, Inc., Newburyport, Massachusetts

Illustration Credits

Cover: Tim Dove, D Childress

Cindy Aarvig–p.20b, 22-24, 25e, 109d-e; Richard Balsam–p. 90c, 97g-h, 145, 149; Barbara Beck–p.75, 77, 87; Scott Bieser–p.146; Antonio Castro (Represented by Cornell & McCarthy, LLC)–p.30, 32d-e, 34, 40a, 42a, 71, 76a, 78a, 82a, 92a, 94, 101, 109a-c; Chris Celusniak–p.51, 69b, 73d-f, 89, 91b-e, 108b-e; Rhonda Childress–p. 137, 142, 143; David Griffin–p.16, 18a, 21b-d, 25a-d, 52, 67, 72a, 99, 100, 107, 114, 116, 148; Dennis Harms–p.32a-c, 60a, 96; Chuck Joseph–p.36, 39d-f, 46b-g, 47b-d, 49d-f; Linda Kelen–p.106; Michael Krone–p.6, 8, 10, 15a-d, 20a, 27, 37, 44a, 44c-d, 46a, 76b-d, 93, 102, 111; Annie Matsick (Represented by Cornell & McCarthy, LLC)–p.28, 29, 33b-g, 64, 68a, 73a-c, 80a, 87, 88, 95; Gordon Ricke–p.63; John Scott–p.11a-b, 56, 58a, 61, 66, 70a, 90a, 91a, 97a-f, 104a, 112, 113b-d; Charles Shaw–p.2, 14, 26, 38, 50, 62, 74, 86, 98, 110; kreativ-design/Danielle Szabo–p.2, 3, 4b-c, 5, 9a-b, 11c-e, 12-14, 15e-h, 18b-e, 21a, 26, 33a, 35, 37e, 38, 39a-c, 40b-c, 42b, 43, 44b, 45, 47a, 48, 49a-c, 50, 53, 55, 57, 58b-c, 59, 60b-c, 62, 68b-e, 70b-d, 72b, 74, 78b, 79, 80b-d, 81, 82b, 83, 84, 85d, 86, 90b, 92b-d, 98, 104b, 105, 108a, 110, 113a, 115, 117-121; Victoria Vebell–p.54.

ISBN 0-8172-7953-9

Copyright © 1999 Steck-Vaughn Company

English ASAP is a trademark of Steck-Vaughn Company.

3 4 5 6 7 8 9 10 DBH 02 01 00 99

Units	Recognition Words
Communication	address ◆ city ◆ first name ◆ last name ◆ name ◆ number ◆ state ◆ street ◆ telephone number ◆ zip code
Your Workplace	bags ◆ bottom ◆ break room ◆ envelopes ◆ exit ◆ gloves ◆ ladies' room ◆ left ◆ men's room ◆ middle ◆ notebooks ◆ office ◆ paper ◆ right ◆ supply room ◆ top ◆ towels
Technology	close ◆ coffee maker ◆ copier ◆ dishwasher ◆ dryer ◆ microwave oven ◆ off ◆ on ◆ open ◆ pull ◆ push ◆ put in ◆ start ◆ stop ◆ take out ◆ vacuum cleaner ◆ washing machine
Time Management	date ◆ date of birth ◆ days of the week ◆ month ◆ months of the year ◆ time ◆ today ◆ tomorrow ◆ year
Customer Service	customer service ◆ exchange ◆ goodbye ◆ hello ◆ please ◆ refund ◆ sorry ◆ thank you
Culture of Work	careful ◆ drive ◆ early ◆ late ◆ on time ◆ quiet ◆ repeat ◆ take ◆ understand ◆ walk ◆ work zone
Finances	cash ◆ cents ◆ change ◆ check ◆ deposit ◆ dime ◆ dollar ◆ ID ◆ nickel ◆ paycheck ◆ penny ◆ quarter ◆ sign ◆ $
Health and Safety	accident ◆ arm ◆ back ◆ broken ◆ cut ◆ danger ◆ emergency room ◆ eye ◆ fire ◆ foot ◆ hand ◆ hospital ◆ hurt ◆ leg ◆ no smoking ◆ poison ◆ 911
Working with People	break ◆ coworkers ◆ good work ◆ lunch ◆ Nice to meet you. ◆ supervisor ◆ Where are you from?
Career Development	application ◆ clerk ◆ cook ◆ custodian ◆ days ◆ experience ◆ full time ◆ help wanted ◆ housekeeper ◆ mechanic ◆ nights ◆ painter ◆ part time ◆ weekends

Introduction to English ASAP

English ASAP is a complete, communicative, SCANS-based, four-skill ESL program for teaching adult and young adult learners the skills they need to succeed at work.

FEATURES

♦ *English ASAP* **is SCANS-based.** *English ASAP*'s SCANS-based syllabus teaches skills learners need to succeed in the workplace. The syllabus is correlated with the SCANS competencies, a taxonomy of work skills recognized by the U.S. Department of Labor as essential to every job. Additionally, the syllabus is compatible with the work skills and competencies in the Comprehensive Adult Student Assessment System (CASAS) Competencies, the Mainstream English Language Training Project (MELT), the National Institute for Literacy's Equipped for the Future Framework for Adult Literacy, and state curriculums for adult ESL from Texas and California.

 The *On Your Job* symbol appears on the Student Book page and corresponding page in the Teacher's Edition each time learners apply a SCANS-based skill to their jobs or career interests.

♦ *English ASAP* **is about the world of work.** All of the conversations, reading selections, listening activities, and realia are drawn from authentic workplace situations. *English ASAP* presents settings and workers from major career clusters, including transportation, health care, service occupations, office occupations, construction, hospitality, and industrial occupations.

♦ *English ASAP* **teaches the skills required in all job descriptions.** Learners gain valuable experience working in teams; teaching others; serving customers; organizing, evaluating, and communicating information; understanding and using technology; negotiating; allocating resources; and completing projects.

♦ *English ASAP* **is communicative.** Numerous conversational models and communicative activities in the Student Books and Teacher's Editions—including problem-solving activities, surveys, and cooperative learning projects—get learners talking from the start.

♦ **English ASAP is appropriate for adults and young adults.** The language and situations presented in *English ASAP* are ones adults and young adults are likely to encounter. The abundance of attractive, true-to-life photographs, illustrations, and realia will interest and motivate adult and young adult learners.

◆ ***English ASAP* addresses all four language skills.** Each level of
English ASAP addresses listening, speaking, reading, and writing.
Starting in Level 1, a two-page grammar spread in each Student Book
unit plus corresponding Workbook reinforcement and supplementary
grammar worksheets in the Teacher's Editions ensure that learners get
appropriate grammar practice.

◆ ***English ASAP* starts at the true beginner level.** *English ASAP* begins
at the Literacy Level, designed for learners who have no prior
knowledge of English and have few or no literacy skills in their native
language(s) or are literate in a language with a non-Roman alphabet.
Learners master foundation literacy skills in tandem with listening and
speaking skills. The next level, Level 1, is intended for learners with
little or no prior knowledge of English. As learners continue through
the program, they master progressively higher levels of language and
work skills. The Placement Tests help teachers place learners in the
appropriate level of the program. For information on placement, see
page v of this Teacher's Edition.

◆ ***English ASAP* is appropriate for multilevel classes.** Because unit topics
carry over from level to level with increasing sophistication, the series is
ideal for use in multilevel classes. For example, a Literacy Level skill in
the technology unit is naming machines. A Level 2 skill in the technology
unit is completing machine maintenance reports. Units are situational and
nonsequential, making *English ASAP* appropriate for open-entry/open-
exit situations.

◆ ***English ASAP* meets the needs of individual workplaces and
learners.** Because the demands of each workplace and each
individual's job are unique, the abundance of *On Your Job* activities
allows learners to relate their new skills to their workplaces and career
interests. In addition, the Personal Dictionary feature in each unit lets
learners focus only on the vocabulary they need to do their jobs.
Finally, with Steck-Vaughn's *Workforce Writing Dictionary,* learners
can create a complete custom dictionary of all the vocabulary they
need to know to succeed.

COMPONENTS

English ASAP consists of:

♦ Student Books

♦ Workbooks starting at Level 1

♦ Teacher's Editions

♦ Audiocassettes

♦ Steck-Vaughn *Workforce Writing Dictionary*

♦ Placement Tests, Form A and Form B

Student Books

Each four-color Student Book consists of ten 12-page units, providing learners with ample time on task to acquire the target SCANS competencies and language.

♦ **The Student Books follow a consistent format for easy teaching and learning.** Each unit is consistently organized and can be taught in approximately eight to twelve classroom sessions.

♦ **Complete front matter offers valuable teaching suggestions.** Ideas on how to teach each type of activity in the Student Book units and suggested teaching techniques give teachers valuable information on how to use *English ASAP* with maximum success.

♦ **Clear directions and abundant examples ensure that learners always know exactly what to do.** Examples for each activity make tasks apparent to learners and teachers. Clear exercise titles and directions tell teachers and learners exactly what learners are to do.

♦ **Performance Check pages provide a complete evaluation program.** Teachers can use these pages to evaluate learners' progress and to track the program's learner verification needs. Success is built in because work skills are always checked in familiar formats.

Workbooks

The Workbooks contain ten eight-page units plus a complete Answer Key. Each Workbook unit always contains at least one exercise for each section of the Student Book. To allow for additional reinforcement of grammar, there are multiple exercises for the Grammar section. The exercises for each section of the Student Book are indicated on the corresponding page of the Teacher's Edition and in a chart at the front of each Workbook. Because the Answer Keys are removable, the Workbooks can be used both in the classroom and for self-study.

Teacher's Editions

The complete Teacher's Editions help both new and experienced teachers organize their teaching, motivate their learners, and successfully use a variety of individual, partner, and teamwork activities.

♦ **Unit Overviews provide valuable information on how to motivate learners and organize teaching.** Each opener contains a complete list of the SCANS and workplace skills in the unit to help teachers organize their teaching. The Unit Warm-Up on each unit opener page helps teachers build learners' interest and gets them ready for the unit. The openers also contain a list of materials—including pictures, flash cards, and realia—teachers can use to enliven instruction throughout the unit.

♦ **The Teacher's Editions contain complete suggested preparation and teaching procedures for each section of the Student Book.** Each section of a unit begins with a list of the workplace skills developed on the Student Book page(s). Teachers can use the list when planning lessons. The teaching notes give suggestions for a recommended three-part lesson format:

Preparation: Suggestions for preteaching the new language, SCANS skills, and concepts on the Student Book page(s) before learners open their books.

Presentation: Suggested procedures for working with the Student Book page(s) in class.

Follow-Up: An optional activity to provide reinforcement or to enrich and extend the new language and competencies. The Follow-Ups include a variety of interactive partner and team activities. Each activity has a suggested variant, marked with ♦ for use with learners who require activities at a slightly more sophisticated level. For teaching ease, the corresponding Workbook exercise(s) for each page or section of the Student Book are indicated on the Teacher's Edition page starting at Level 1.

♦ **The Teacher's Editions contain SCANS Notes, Teaching Notes, Culture Notes, and Language Notes.** Teachers can share this wealth of information with learners or use it in lesson planning.

♦ **Each Teacher's Edition unit contains an additional suggested Informal Workplace-Specific Assessment.** Teachers will find these suggestions invaluable in evaluating learners' success in relating their new skills to their workplaces or career interests. Designed to supplement the Performance Check pages in each unit of the Student

Books, these brief speaking activities include having learners state their workplace's customer service policies, their workplace's policies on lateness and absence, and the procedures they use at work to maintain equipment.

♦ **Blackline Masters.** In the Literacy Level, the Blackline Masters help teachers present or reinforce many basic literacy skills. Starting at Level 1, the Blackline Masters reinforce the grammar in each unit.

♦ **Additional features in the Teacher's Editions.** The Teacher's Editions contain Individual Competency Charts for each unit and a Class Cumulative Competency Chart for recording learners' progress and tracking the program's learner verification needs. A Certificate of Completion is included for teachers to copy and award to learners upon successful completion of that level of *English ASAP*. In addition, each unit of the Literacy Level Teacher's Edition contains an ASAP Project, an optional holistic cooperative learning project. Learners will find these to be valuable and stimulating culminating activities. Starting at Level 1, the ASAP Project appears directly on the Student Book pages.

Audiocassettes

The audiocassettes contain all the dialogs and listening activities marked with this cassette symbol. The audiocassettes provide experience in listening to a variety of native speakers in the workplace. The Listening Transcript at the back of each Student Book and Teacher's Edition contains the scripts of all the listening selections not appearing directly on the pages of the Student Books.

Workforce Writing Dictionary

The Steck-Vaughn *Workforce Writing Dictionary* is a 96-page custom dictionary that lets learners create a personalized, alphabetical list of words and expressions related to their own workplaces and career interests. Each letter of the alphabet is allocated two to four pages and is illustrated with several workforce-related words. Learners can use the dictionary to record all of the relevant language they need to succeed on their jobs.

Placement Tests

The Placement Tests, Form A and Form B, help teachers place learners in the appropriate level of *English ASAP*. For more information see page v of this Teacher's Edition.

About SCANS

Each unit of *English ASAP* systematically presents one or more SCANS Competencies. The Foundation Skills are integrated through all the instruction.

WORKPLACE KNOW-HOW

The know-how identified by SCANS is made up of five competencies and a three-part foundation of skills and personal qualities needed for solid job performance. These include:

COMPETENCIES—effective workers can productively use:

- **Resources**—allocating time, money, materials, space, staff;

- **Interpersonal Skills**—working on teams, teaching others, serving customers, leading, negotiating, and working well with people from culturally diverse backgrounds;

- **Information**—acquiring and evaluating data, organizing and maintaining files, interpreting and communicating, and using computers to process information;

- **Systems**—understanding social, organizational, and technological systems, monitoring and correcting performance, and designing or improving systems;

- **Technology**—selecting equipment and tools, applying technology to specific tasks, and maintaining and troubleshooting technologies.

THE FOUNDATION—competence requires:

- **Basic Skills**—reading, writing, arithmetic and mathematics, speaking and listening;

- **Thinking Skills**—thinking creatively, making decisions, solving problems, seeing things in the mind's eye, knowing how to learn, and reasoning;

- **Personal Qualities**—individual responsibility, self-esteem, sociability, self-management, and integrity.

Reprinted from *What Work Requires of Schools—A SCANS Report for America 2000,* Secretary's Commission on Achieving Necessary Skills, U.S. Department of Labor.

For Additional Information

For more information on SCANS, CASAS, adult literacy, and the workforce, visit these websites.

CASAS Information

www.casas.org

Center for Applied Linguistics

www.cal.org

Education Information

www.ed.gov

Literacy Link

www.pbs.org/learn/literacy

National Center for Adult Literacy

www.literacyonline.org/ncal/index.html

National Institute for Literacy

novel.nifl.gov

School-to-Work Information

www.stw.ed.gov

Workforce Information

www.doleta.gov

For more information about Steck-Vaughn, visit our website.

www.steckvaughn.com

Steck-Vaughn

English ASAP™

Connecting English to the Workplace

SCANS Consultant

Andrea Perrault
Connected Resources—Learning that Works!
Boston, Massachusetts

Program Consultants

Judith Dean-Griffin
ESL Teacher
Windham Independent School District
Texas Department of Criminal Justice
Huntsville, Texas

Marilyn K. Spence
Workforce Education Coordinator
Orange Technical Education Centers
Mid-Florida Tech
Orlando, Florida

Brigitte Marshall
English Language Training
for Employment Participation
Albany, California

Dennis Terdy
Director, Community Education
Township High School District 214
Arlington Heights, Illinois

Christine Kay Williams
ESL Specialist
Towson University
Baltimore, Maryland

STECK-VAUGHN®
C O M P A N Y

A Division of Harcourt Brace & Company

About SCANS, the Workforce, and *English ASAP: Connecting English to the Workplace*

SCANS and the Workforce

The Secretary's Commission on Achieving Necessary Skills (SCANS) was established by the U.S. Department of Labor in 1990. Its mission was to study the demands of workplace environments and determine whether people entering the workforce are capable of meeting those demands. The commission identified skills for employment, suggested ways for assessing proficiency, and devised strategies to implement the identified skills. This commission's first report, entitled *What Work Requires of Schools—SCANS Report for America 2000*, was published in June 1991. The report is designed for use by educators (curriculum developers, job counselors, training directors, and teachers) to prepare the modern workforce for the workplace with viable, up-to-date skills.

The report identified two types of skills: Competencies and Foundations. There are five SCANS Competencies: (1) Resources, (2) Interpersonal, (3) Information, (4) Systems, and (5) Technology. There are three parts contained in SCANS Foundations: (1) Basic Skills (including reading, writing, arithmetic, mathematics, listening, and speaking); (2) Thinking Skills (including creative thinking, decision making, problem solving, seeing things in the mind's eye, knowing how to learn, and reasoning); and (3) Personal Qualities (including responsibility, self-esteem, sociability, self-management, and integrity/honesty).

Steck-Vaughn's *English ASAP: Connecting English to the Workplace*

English ASAP is a complete SCANS-based, four-skills program for teaching ESL and SCANS skills to adults and young adults. *English ASAP* follows a work skills–based syllabus that is compatible with work skills in the CASAS and MELT competencies. The program has these components:

Student Books

The Student Books are designed to allow from 125 to 235 hours of instruction. Each Student Book contains 10 units of SCANS-based instruction. A Listening Transcript of material appearing on the Audiocassettes and a Vocabulary list, organized by unit, of core workforce-based words and phrases appear at the back of each Student Book. Because unit topics carry over from level to level, *English ASAP* is ideal for multilevel classes.

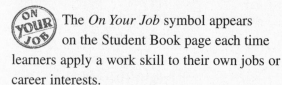 The *On Your Job* symbol appears on the Student Book page each time learners apply a work skill to their own jobs or career interests.

Teacher's Editions

The Teacher's Editions provide reduced Student Book pages with answers inserted and wraparound teacher notes that give detailed suggestions on how to present each page of the Student Book in class. Teacher's Editions 1 and 2 also provide Blackline Masters to reinforce the grammar in each unit. The Literacy Level Teacher's Edition contains Blackline Masters that provide practice with many basic literacy skills. The complete Listening Transcript,

Vocabulary list, charts for tracking individual and class success, and a Certificate of Completion appear at the back of each Teacher's Edition.

Workbooks

The Workbooks, starting at Level 1, provide reinforcement for each section of the Student Books.

Audiocassettes

The Audiocassettes contain all the dialogs and listening activities in the Student Books.

 This symbol appears on the Student Book page and corresponding Teacher's Edition page each time material for that page is recorded on the Audiocassettes. A Listening Transcript of all material recorded on the tapes but not appearing directly on the Student Book pages is at the back of each Student Book and Teacher's Edition.

Workforce Writing Dictionary

Steck-Vaughn's *Workforce Writing Dictionary* is a 96-page custom dictionary that allows learners to create a personalized, alphabetical list of the key words and phrases they need to know for their jobs. Each letter of the alphabet is allocated two to four pages for learners to record the language they need. In addition, each letter is illustrated with several workforce-related words.

Placement Tests

The Placement Tests, Form A and Form B, can be used as entry and exit tests and to assist in placing learners in the appropriate level of *English ASAP.*

Placement

In addition to the Placement Tests, the following table indicates placement based on the CASAS and new MELT student performance level standards.

Placement

New MELT SPL	CASAS Achievement Score	English ASAP
0–1	179 or under	Literacy
2–3	180–200	Level 1
4–5	201–220	Level 2
6	221-235	Level 3
7	236 and above	Level 4

Using this Book in Multilevel Classes

English ASAP Literacy Level can be used in a variety of ways in multilevel classes. Here is a suggested procedure.

◆ Present to the class as a whole the oral and aural activities for the day in Level 1 of *English ASAP.*

◆ Meet with the literacy learners as a group for the reading and writing instruction in the Literacy Level Student Book as the Level 1 learners complete the exercises in their Student Books and Workbooks.

◆ When the literacy learners are ready to begin the independent or paired activities in their books, check the Level 1 learners' work or provide them with additional instruction.

About the Literacy Level

Organization of a Unit

Each of the ten units follows a consistent whole-part-whole organization.

◆ The Unit Opener's illustrations and accompanying questions introduce the unit topic and preview the SCANS skills covered in the unit.

◆ The Getting Started page uses interactive activities and peer teaching to introduce the new language in the unit.

- Four teaching spreads systematically present the new material in the unit.

- The Extension page allows for integration and expansion of the new language, literacy skills, and SCANS skills.

- The Performance Check page allows teachers to assess learners' progress and to determine whether any additional reinforcement is needed.

Unit Opener

Each Unit Opener includes four large, engaging illustrations and accompanying questions. Each illustration depicts people using the unit's target language, literacy skills, and SCANS skills. Situations include people applying for jobs, completing forms, interacting with coworkers and supervisors, using technology at work, and assisting customers. The illustrations and questions activate learners' prior knowledge by getting them to think and talk about the unit topic. To stimulate discussion, follow these suggestions:

- Encourage learners to say whatever they can about the illustrations. Prompt them by indicating objects for them to name. You might also identify and say the names of objects, places, and people for them to point to and repeat. Write key words on the board.

- Help learners read any signs or words that are visible.

- Have learners answer the questions. Repeat their answers or restate them in acceptable English.

Getting Started

An initial teamwork activity presents the key work skills, concepts, and language introduced in the unit. Critical thinking and peer teaching activities activate the use of the new language and preview the content of the unit. A partner work activity encourages learners to use the new language in communicative ways.

Teaching Spreads

Each of the four teaching spreads presents one or more literacy skill and SCANS skill. *English ASAP* Literacy Level takes a recognition-word approach to teach letters and words in meaningful, communicative contexts. Learners learn to read and write only the words that they need to master the unit SCANS skills.

- The recognition words for each spread are presented at the top of the first page of that spread. For information on presenting recognition words, see "Presenting Recognition Words" on page viii.

- The first activity on each spread is usually a short dialog that presents the spread's recognition words in context. As learners listen to and say each dialog, they gain valuable experience using the new language. For detailed instructions, see "Presenting Dialogs" on page viii.

- Exercises give learners experience in reading and writing the recognition words in isolation and in context.

- The complete alphabet is presented in the first six units. The letters are usually included in the spread's recognition words. Thus, learning the alphabet becomes a meaningful, relevant task. Exercises give learners experience in writing letters in isolation and in the context of familiar SCANS-based words. For suggestions on teaching the letters, see "Presenting Letters" on page ix.

- Listening and speaking activities appear throughout the teaching spreads, allowing learners to develop all four language skills. The paired speaking activities get learners talking from the start. Listening tasks include listening for addresses, telephone numbers, names of work supplies, locations, days of the week, dates, times, and prices.

All of the listening activities develop the skill of **focused listening.** Learners learn to recognize the information they need and to listen selectively for only that information. They do not have to understand every word;

To the Teacher

rather, they have to filter out everything except the relevant information. This essential skill is used by native speakers of all languages when listening to their own languages.

♦ Culminating activities on each spread allow learners to use their new literacy skills, and include reading or filling in pieces of realia such as job applications or checks, practicing dialogs, and completing writing activities.

Extension

Following the teaching spreads, the Extension page enriches the previous instruction. As in other sections, realia is used extensively. Oral and written exercises help learners master additional skills, language, and concepts, and relate them to their workplaces and career interests.

Performance Check

Each unit concludes with a one-page Performance Check, which is designed to allow teachers to track learners' progress and to meet their school's or program's learner verification needs. Skills are tested in the same manner that they are presented in the units, so formats are familiar and nonthreatening, and success is built in. For more information on this section, see "Evaluation" on page ix.

Teaching Techniques

Make Your Classroom Mirror the Workplace

Help learners develop workplace skills by setting up your classroom to mirror a workplace. Use any of these suggestions.

♦ Establish policies on lateness and absence similar to those a business might have.

♦ Provide learners with a daily agenda of the activities they will complete that day, including partner work and small group assignments. Go over the agenda with learners at the beginning and end of class.

♦ With learner input, establish a list of goals for the class. Goals can include speaking, reading, and writing English every day; using effective teamwork skills; or learning ten new vocabulary words every unit. Go over the goals with learners at regular intervals.

♦ Assign regular jobs and responsibilities to learners, such as arranging the chairs in a circle, setting up the overhead projector, or making copies for the class.

Presenting a Unit Opener

The unit opener sets the stage for the unit. Use the illustrations and questions to encourage learners to speculate about what the unit might cover, activate prior knowledge, and relate what they see in the illustrations to their own work environments.

Peer Teaching

Because each adult learner brings rich life experience to the classroom, *English ASAP* is designed to help you use each learner's expertise as a resource for peer teaching.

Here are some practical strategies for peer teaching:

♦ Have learners work in pairs/small groups to clarify new language concepts for each other.

♦ If a learner possesses a particular work skill, appoint that learner as "class consultant" in that area and have learners direct queries to that individual.

♦ Set up a reference area in a corner of your classroom. Include dictionaries, career books, and other books your learners will find useful.

Partner Work and Teamwork

The abundance of partner work and teamwork activities in *English ASAP* serves the dual purposes of developing learners' communicative competence and providing learners with experience using key SCANS interpersonal skills, such as working in teams, teaching others, leading, negotiating, and working well with people from culturally diverse backgrounds. To take full advantage of these activities, follow these suggestions.

♦ Whenever learners work in groups, appoint, or have learners select, a leader.

♦ Use multiple groupings. Have learners work with different partners and teams, just as workers do in the workplace. For different activities, you might group learners according to language ability, work skill, or learner interest.

♦ Make sure learners understand that everyone on the team is responsible for the team's work.

♦ At the end of each activity, have teams report the results to the class.

♦ Discuss with learners their teamwork skills and talk about ways teams can work together effectively. They can discuss how to clarify roles and responsibilities, resolve disagreements effectively, communicate openly, and make decisions together.

Presenting Dialogs

To present the dialogs, follow these suggested steps.

♦ Establish meaning by having learners talk about the illustration. Clarify all the new vocabulary in the dialog using pictures and pantomime.

♦ Play the tape or say the dialog aloud two or more times.

♦ Say the dialog aloud line-by-line for learners to repeat chorally and then individually.

♦ Have learners say the dialog together in pairs.

♦ Have several pairs say the dialog aloud for the class.

Presenting Recognition Words

To present each recognition word, first clarify the meaning of the word. Display the object or a picture card, or use the picture on the Student Book page. Say the word and have learners repeat. Then display a word card with the word on it. Say the word. As you say it, sweep your hand under the word. Have learners repeat. Display the word card and the picture card at random and have the class say or read the word chorally each time. Continue until the class can respond with ease. Then have individuals respond.

Reinforcing Vocabulary

To provide additional reinforcement of the recognition words, use any of these suggestions.

♦ **Steck-Vaughn's *Workforce Writing Dictionary.*** Learners can use Steck-Vaughn's *Workforce Writing Dictionary* to create a completely customized lexicon of key words and phrases they need to know.

♦ **Flash cards.** Flash cards are easy for you or your learners to make. Write a new word or phrase on the front of each card. Put a picture of the object or action on the back of the card. Learners can use the cards to review vocabulary or to play a variety of games, such as Concentration.

♦ **The Remember-It Game.** Use this simple memory game to review the vocabulary of any topic. For example, to reinforce names of places at work, start the game by saying, *We're going to the office.* The next learner has to repeat what you said and add a place. For example, he or she may say, *We're going to the office and the break room.* If someone cannot remember the whole list or cannot add a word, he or she has to drop out. The learner who can remember the longest list wins.

To the Teacher

Presenting Letters

Use letter cards with both capital and lower-case letters on them to present the letters. Hold up each card, say the name of the letter, and have learners repeat. Point out the difference between capital and lower-case letters. Write the capital and lower-case letters on the board and trace them with your finger. Have learners trace the strokes in the air. Next, have learners open their books and trace the letters with their fingers and with their pencils. Then have them write the letters on the lines. Use Blackline Masters 2, 3, and 5 in the Teacher's Edition to provide additional reinforcement.

Environmental Print

As learners learn new letters, encourage them to find examples of the new letters in the room around them. You might ask them to find examples in old magazines, in items in their purses or wallets (such as driver's licenses or work permits), on signs in the room, or on objects visible from the window.

Presenting Listening Activities

Use any of these suggestions to present the listening activities.

♦ Help learners read the directions.

♦ Model the activity. Write the example item on the board and complete it as you play the tape or read the Listening Transcript of the first item aloud.

♦ Play the tape or read the Listening Transcript aloud as learners complete the activity. Rewind the tape and play it again as necessary.

♦ Check learners' work.

Evaluation

To use the Performance Check page successfully, follow these suggested procedures:

Before and during each evaluation, create a relaxed, affirming atmosphere. Chat with the learners for a few minutes and review the material with them. Make sure that everyone has a pen or a pencil. When you and the learners are ready, help learners read the directions and look over each exercise before they complete it. Then have learners complete the activity. If at any time during the process you sense that the learners are becoming frustrated, feel free to stop the evaluation process to provide additional review. You might have learners turn back to the page where the material was presented. Resume when learners are ready. Check learners' work. The Teacher's Edition contains reproducible charts for you to copy and use to keep track of individual and class progress.

To the Teacher

Steck-Vaughn

English ASAP™

Connecting English to the Workplace

Unit 1 Overview

—SCANS Competencies—

★ Communicate information

★ Acquire and interpret information

Unit 1 Workforce Skills

- Understand a simple form
- Ask for and give personal information
- Introduce oneself
- Complete a simple form

Materials

- Letter cards for **n, a, c,** and **t**
- Number cards for **0** through **10**
- Word cards for **name, first name, last name, address, number, street, city, state, zip code,** and **telephone number**
- A name card with your first and last names on it and a name card for each learner
- Realia: a picture of your family or friends, envelopes addressed to you, blank envelopes, sheets of paper, simple personal information forms such as job applications and W-4 forms, a telephone, a telephone directory, and identification tags (such as luggage tags or storage box labels)
- Blackline Masters: 2, 3, 4, 5, 8, and 10

★   ★   ★   ★   ★

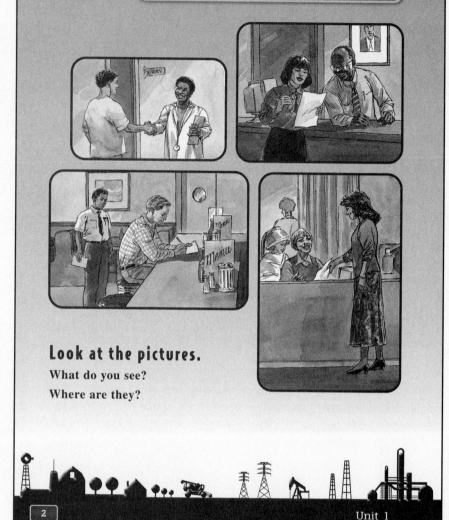

UNIT 1 Communication

Look at the pictures.

What do you see?

Where are they?

2   Unit 1

WORKFORCE SKILLS (page 2)

Ask for and give personal information

★   ★   ★   ★   ★

Teaching Note

Use Blackline Masters 6 and 7: Common Directions to clarify the directions in this unit. Use page 2 to warm up learners, to draw on prior knowledge, and to spark interest.

PREPARATION

Begin the class by introducing yourself and having learners introduce themselves to you and each other. If necessary, teach them how to ask other people's names and tell other people their own names. Follow these suggestions.

- Hold up the card with your name on it. Say, *My name is (name).* Have learners repeat with their names.

PRESENTATION

Focus attention on the illustrations. Have learners say as much as they can about them. Learners may be able to name a few objects, but you may have to prompt them by naming items, places, and occupations and having learners repeat. You also might read the unit title and questions aloud and have learners answer the questions.

FOLLOW-UP

Learning Each Other's Names: Have the class sit in a circle. Ask the person beside you to say his or her name aloud.

Then say, *My name is (name), and this is (name of person beside you).* Each person, in turn, says his or her own name and tries to recall and say the names of the people who have already given their names.

♦ Have learners change seats and repeat the activity.

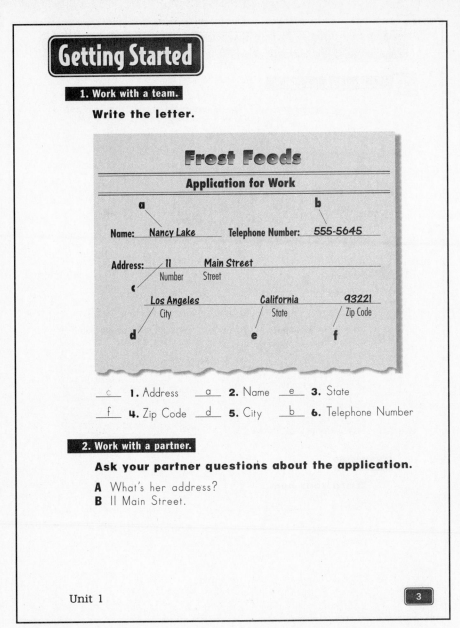

Getting Started

1. Work with a team.

Write the letter.

Frost Foods

Application for Work

a

Name: <u>Nancy Lake</u> **b** Telephone Number: <u>555-5645</u>

Address: <u>11</u> <u>Main Street</u>
      Number   Street
c

  <u>Los Angeles</u>   <u>California</u>   <u>93221</u>
   City   State   Zip Code
d   **e**   **f**

<u>c</u> **1.** Address   <u>a</u> **2.** Name   <u>e</u> **3.** State

<u>f</u> **4.** Zip Code   <u>d</u> **5.** City   <u>b</u> **6.** Telephone Number

2. Work with a partner.

Ask your partner questions about the application.

A What's her address?
B 11 Main Street.

Unit 1

`3`

Teaching Note

Use this page to introduce the new language in the unit. Whenever possible, encourage peer teaching. Supply any language the learners need.

PREPARATION

Display addressed envelopes and simple personal information forms or Blackline Master 8: Identification Forms. Allow learners to identify or comment on information that they recognize, such as parts of the address.

Preteach the new words in the lesson. Follow these suggestions.

● To teach the word **name,** hold up the word card for **name** and say, *My name is (first and last names).* Have learners repeat, using their own names. See "Presenting Recognition Words" on page viii.

● Introduce **address, number, street, city, state,** and **zip code.** Write the school's or workplace's address on the board or overhead projector. Say, *This is (the school's) address.* Continue similarly with the other words. You also may want to use simple drawings to convey the meanings of the words.

● Introduce the word cards for **address, city, state, zip code,** and **telephone number.** Say the words as you indicate the address and its parts. Have learners repeat. Hold up one of the word cards, have a volunteer read it and indicate the appropriate item in the address on the board. Repeat until learners can do this easily. See "Presenting Recognition Words" on page viii.

PRESENTATION

1. Help learners read the directions. Demonstrate by completing the first item on the board or overhead projector. Have learners complete the exercise in teams. Go over the answers with the class.

2. Help learners read the directions. Model the dialog as learners listen. Say the dialog again and have learners repeat. Ask learners to practice the dialog with a partner. Then model substituting the next item on the page in the dialog, and ask learners to continue similarly with the remaining items.

FOLLOW-UP

Point To It: Say the target words and have learners point to the words on the application.

♦ Bring in samples of job applications or other personal information forms and have pairs of learners find the target words on them.

WORKFORCE SKILLS (pages 4-5)

Ask for and give personal information

Introduce oneself

★   ★   ★   ★   ★

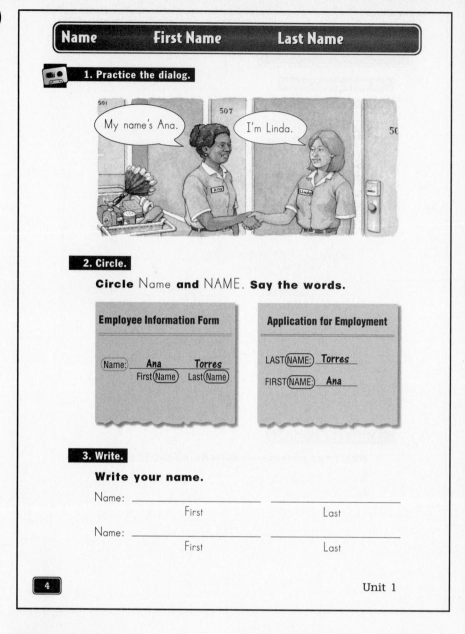

PREPARATION

Preteach or review the new language in the lesson. Follow these suggestions.

● Review introductions. Follow the instructions on page 2.

● Introduce or review **name.** Follow the procedure on page 3.

● Say, *What is your name?* and hold up the word card for **name.** Then hold up the name card for a volunteer and prompt him or her to say his or her name. Repeat with other learners.

● Follow the same suggestions for **first name** and **last name.**

PRESENTATION

1. Focus attention on the illustration. Help learners read the speech balloons. Have learners say as much as they can about the illustration. You may want to cue them by saying names of items and having learners point to them. Restate learners' ideas in acceptable English and write them on the board or overhead projector. Identify the women as Ana and Linda. Write their names on the board.

Present the dialog. See "Presenting Dialogs" on page viii.

2. Help learners read the directions. Demonstrate by circling **Name** on the board or overhead projector and then reading the word aloud. Then have learners complete the exercise in pairs.

Check each learner's work and provide feedback as needed.

3. Help learners read the directions. Demonstrate on the board or overhead projector by filling in the blank with your name. If necessary, show individuals how to write their names. Have learners write or copy their first and last names in their books. Check their work individually, giving feedback and assistance as needed.

4. Help learners read the directions. Then present the listening activity. See "Presenting Listening Activities" on page ix. Check learners' work. Ask volunteers to read their answers aloud.

5. Present or review the letter **n.** See "Presenting Letters" on page ix. Then have learners complete the exercise.

4. Listen.

Circle the word you hear.

a. first (last)   b. (name) first

c. first (last)   d. last (first)

5. Write.

Write the letter. Say the letter. Say the words.

N n

N n

___N__ame   _____ame   _____ame   _____ame

___n__ame   _____ame   _____ame   _____ame

6. Write.

Write your name.

Employee Information Form

Name: _____   _____
           First Name   Last Name

Application for Work

_____   _____
Last Name   First Name

Check learners' work. For extra reinforcement, use Blackline Master 3: Alphabet N-Z and Blackline Master 5: Lined Paper.

Environmental Print: Have learners point out examples of words with **N** and **n** they see in the room. For more information, see "Environmental Print" on page ix.

6. Help learners read the directions. Demonstrate by completing the first item about yourself on the board or overhead projector. Then ask learners to complete the exercise independently. Have them check each other's work in pairs and read their names aloud to each other and then to the class.

FOLLOW-UP

First Names First: Have learners bring in pictures of family members or of one or two other people they know. Or have them draw stick figures of themselves and one other person. Then have learners select partners and tell the first names and last names of the people in the pictures or drawings. Have learners change partners and repeat the activity. Encourage volunteers to show their pictures to the class and tell the first and last names of the people.

♦ Have learners write the first and last names of each person under the stick figures.

WORKFORCE SKILLS (pages 6-7)

Ask for and give personal information

Complete a simple form

★　　★　　★　　★　　★

1. Practice the dialog.

> What's your address?

> 10 Park Street.

2. Write.

Write your address.

Address: _____
　　　　　Number　　　Street

Address: _____
　　　　　Number　　　Street

3. Listen.

Circle the word you hear.

a.　(address)　　name　　number

b.　name　　street　　(number)

c.　address　　(street)　　name

d.　(address)　　street　　number

6　　　　　　　　　　　　　　　　　　Unit 1

Teaching Note

Learners may not want to reveal their addresses and telephone numbers in class. If so, they should use fictitious addresses and telephone numbers.

PREPARATION

Preteach or review the new language in the lesson. Follow these suggestions.

● Preteach or review the numerals **0** through **10.** Use flash cards to identify each number. Hold up the flash card and say the number. Have learners repeat. Demonstrate writing the numbers on the board or overhead projector. Then have learners copy the numbers. Check each learner's work and provide immediate feedback. For extra reinforcement, use Blackline Master 4: Numbers and Blackline Master 5: Lined Paper.

● Introduce or review **address, number,** and **street.** Follow the procedure on page 3. Then point to the number on the board or screen and on the envelope and say, *This is the number.* Repeat for the street.

● One by one, introduce or review the word cards for **address, number,** and **street.** Follow the procedure on page 3.

PRESENTATION

1. Focus attention on the illustration. Help learners read the speech balloons. Have learners say as much as they can about the illustration. You may want to cue them by indicating the items and having learners say the names, or by saying names of items and having learners indicate them. Restate their ideas in acceptable English and write them on the board or overhead projector.

Present the dialog. See "Presenting Dialogs" on page viii.

2. Present or review writing numerals **0** through **10.** For extra reinforcement, use Blackline Master 4: Numbers. Then help learners read the directions. Demonstrate by completing the first item on the board. If necessary, show individuals how to write their addresses. Write each learner's address on a card or in his or her book. Have learners complete the exercise independently. Check learners' work and provide feedback as necessary.

3. Help learners read the directions. Then present the listening activity. See "Presenting Listening Activities" on page ix. Check learners' work. Ask volunteers to read their answers aloud.

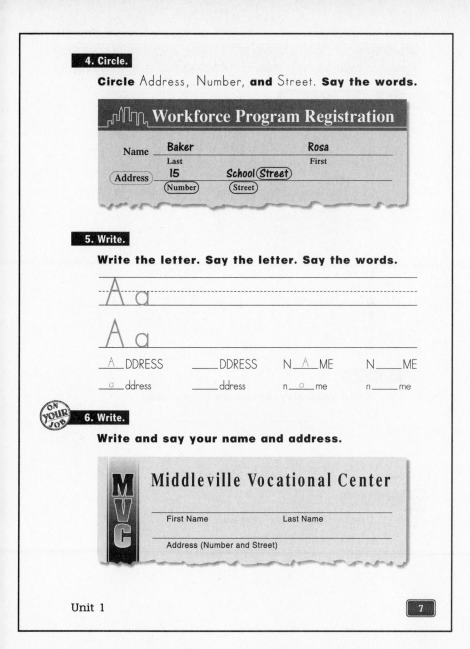

4. Circle.

Circle Address, Number, **and** Street. **Say the words.**

Workforce Program Registration

Name   Baker   Rosa
       Last   First
(Address)   15   School (Street)
        (Number)   (Street)

5. Write.

Write the letter. Say the letter. Say the words.

A a

A a

_A_DDRESS   ____DDRESS   N_A_ME   N____ME
_a_ ddress   ____ ddress   n_a_ me   n____ me

 6. Write.

Write and say your name and address.

Middleville Vocational Center

First Name   Last Name

Address (Number and Street)

4. Help learners read the directions. Demonstrate by completing the first item on the board or overhead projector and reading the word aloud. Then have learners complete the exercise independently. Check each learner's work and provide feedback.

5. Present or review the letter **a.** See "Presenting Letters" on page ix. Then have learners complete the exercise. Check learners' work. For extra reinforcement, use Blackline Master 2: Alphabet A-M and Blackline Master 5: Lined Paper.

Environmental Print: Have learners point out examples of words with **A** and **a** they see in the room. For more information, see "Environmental Print" on page ix.

6. Help learners read the directions. Demonstrate by completing the first item on the board or overhead projector. Have learners complete the exercise independently. Check learners' work. Then have learners practice reading aloud their names and addresses with partners.

FOLLOW-UP

What's Your Address? Write a name and address on the board. Say words and phrases from the unit, such as **first name** or **street.** Have learners point to the corresponding information on the board. Other learners should watch and make sure their classmates point to the correct information. Repeat the activity with several different learners.

♦ Have learners fold a sheet of paper in half, then in half again the other way to form four boxes. Instruct learners to ask four different classmates to write their names and addresses. Classmates respond by writing the information in the boxes.

WORKFORCE SKILLS (pages 8-9)

Ask for and give personal information

Complete a simple form

★   ★   ★   ★   ★

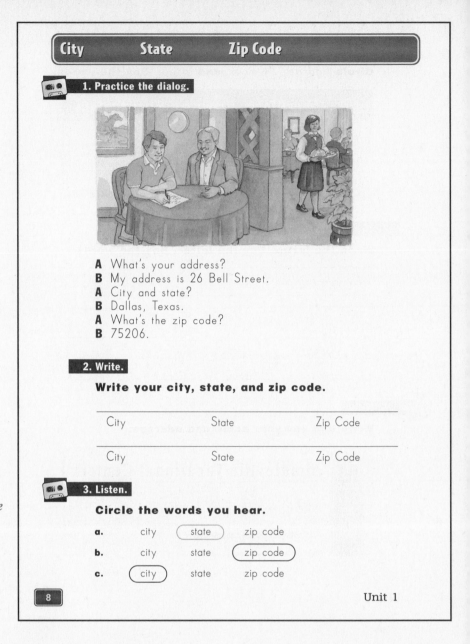

| City | State | Zip Code |

1. Practice the dialog.

A What's your address?
B My address is 26 Bell Street.
A City and state?
B Dallas, Texas.
A What's the zip code?
B 75206.

2. Write.

Write your city, state, and zip code.

City	State	Zip Code

City	State	Zip Code

3. Listen.

Circle the words you hear.

a.   city   (state)   zip code

b.   city   state   (zip code)

c.   (city)   state   zip code

8   Unit 1

Language Note

Explain that zip codes are usually read one number at a time. Tell learners that the numeral 0 is usually pronounced like the letter o.

PREPARATION

Preteach or review the new language in the lesson. Follow these suggestions.

● Review **city** and **state.** Follow the procedure on page 3. Say, *I live in (city and state).*

● To review **zip code,** show learners an envelope mailed to you. Point out the zip code and explain that it is an important part of a mailing address. Add the zip code to the school's or workplace's address on the board or overhead projector. If your learners have different zip codes, write these on the board or overhead projector, too. Indicate parts of the addresses and have volunteers tell you if they are the city, state, or zip code.

● One at a time, hold up word cards for **city, state,** and **zip code.** Say the words and have learners repeat. Call attention to the initial consonant in each word. Hold up one of the word cards, have a volunteer read it, and indicate the appropriate item in your school's or workplace's address on the board or overhead projector. Repeat until learners can do this easily. See "Presenting Recognition Words" on page viii.

PRESENTATION

 1. Focus attention on the illustration. Have learners say as much as they can about it. You may wish to cue them by indicating the items and having learners say the names, or by saying names of items and having learners indicate them.

Restate their ideas in acceptable English and write them on the board or overhead projector.

Present the dialog. See "Presenting Dialogs" on page viii.

2. Help learners read the directions. Demonstrate by completing a model on the board. Write each learner's city, state, and zip code on a card or in his or her book. Have learners complete the exercise independently. Check learners' work and provide feedback as necessary.

 3. Help learners read the directions. Then present the listening activity. See "Presenting Listening Activities" on page ix. Check learners' work. Ask volunteers to read their answers aloud.

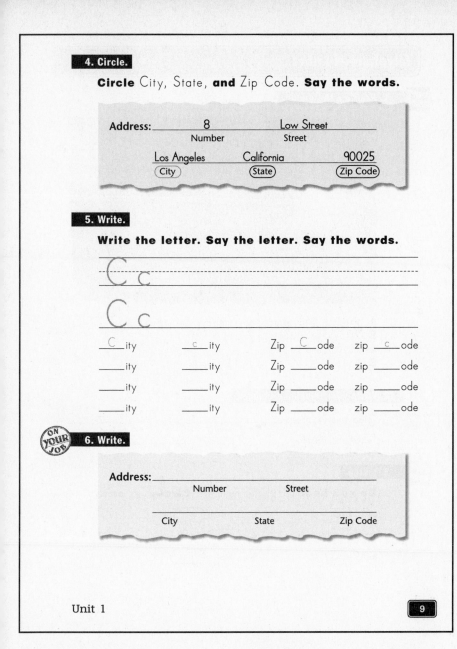

4. Circle.

Circle City, State, **and** Zip Code. **Say the words.**

Address: _____8_____ _____Low Street_____
Number Street

Los Angeles California 90025
(City) (State) (Zip Code)

5. Write.

Write the letter. Say the letter. Say the words.

C c

C c

C__ity   c__ity   Zip C__ode   zip c__ode
___ity   ___ity   Zip ___ode   zip ___ode
___ity   ___ity   Zip ___ode   zip ___ode
___ity   ___ity   Zip ___ode   zip ___ode

 6. Write.

Address: _____
Number Street

City State Zip Code

SCANS Note

If your learners have trouble filling out forms neatly and accurately, tell them to ask for two copies of the forms they complete. Tell them to fill out and check one copy of the form as a rough draft. Then learners can copy the information onto a final version of the form.

4. Help learners read the directions. Demonstrate by circling **City** on the board or overhead projector and reading the word aloud. Then have learners complete the exercise in pairs. Check the exercise on the board or overhead projector. Ask volunteers to read the words aloud.

5. Present or review the letter **c.** See "Presenting Letters" on page ix. Then have learners complete the exercise. Check learners' work. For extra reinforcement, use Blackline Master 2: Alphabet A-M and Blackline Master 5: Lined Paper.

Environmental Print: Have learners point out examples of words with **C** and **c** they see in the room. For more information, see "Environmental Print" on page ix.

6. Help learners read the directions. Demonstrate by filling in the form on the board or overhead projector. Then have learners work in pairs to help each other complete the exercise. Check learners' work. Ask volunteers to read their answers aloud.

FOLLOW-UP

Interviews: Have pairs of learners interview each other. First demonstrate the activity with a volunteer. Ask, *What's your address? What's your city? What's your state? What's your zip code?* To help learners remember the questions, write the words **address, city, state,** and **zip code** on the board or overhead projector. Then have learners complete the activity.

♦ Provide each learner with an envelope. Help learners practice addressing their envelopes to themselves. You may want to collect the envelopes and use them to send class information or short notes to learners.

WORKFORCE SKILLS (pages 10-11)

Ask for and give personal information

Complete a simple form

★   ★   ★   ★   ★

Culture Note

If in your city an area code is required for local calls, make sure learners know to include it when they give their telephone numbers.

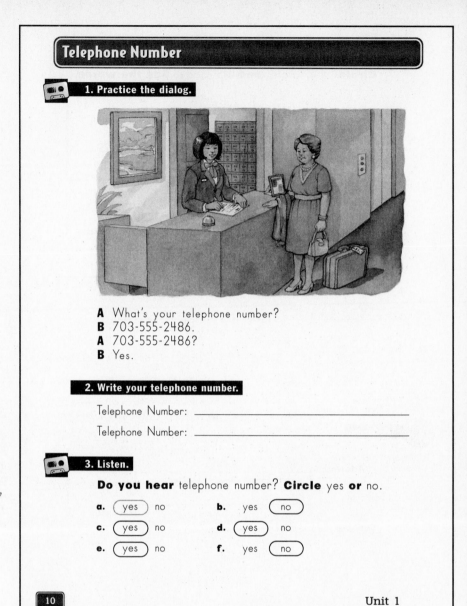

PREPARATION

Preteach the new language in the lesson. Follow these suggestions.

● Review the numerals **0** through **10.** Follow the instructions on page 6.

● Show learners a real telephone or Blackline Master 10: Telephone. Indicate the numerals on the phone and have learners say the numbers as you point to them.

● Write the school's or workplace's telephone number on the board or overhead projector. Say, *Our school's (or This company's) telephone number is (telephone number).* Ask volunteers to say their telephone numbers.

● Hold up the word card for **telephone number,** read the words and have learners repeat them. Call attention to the initial

consonant in each word. Hold up the word card again and ask a volunteer to write his or her telephone number on the board or overhead projector. See "Presenting Recognition Words" on page viii.

PRESENTATION

 1. Focus attention on the illustration. Have learners say as much as they can about it. You may want to cue them by indicating the items and having learners say the names, or by saying names of items and having learners indicate them. Restate their ideas in acceptable English and write them on the board or overhead projector.

Present the dialog. See "Presenting Dialogs" on page viii.

2. Help learners read the directions. Demonstrate by filling in your tele-

phone number on the board or overhead projector. Write each learner's telephone number on a card or in his or her book. Have learners complete the exercise independently. Check learners' work and provide feedback as necessary.

 3. Help learners read the directions. Then present the listening activity. See "Presenting Listening Activities" on page ix. Check learners' work. Ask volunteers to read their answers aloud.

4. Present or review the letter **t.** See "Presenting Letters" on page ix. Then have learners complete the exercise. Check learners' work. For extra reinforcement, use Blackline Master 3: Alphabet N-Z and Blackline Master 5: Lined Paper.

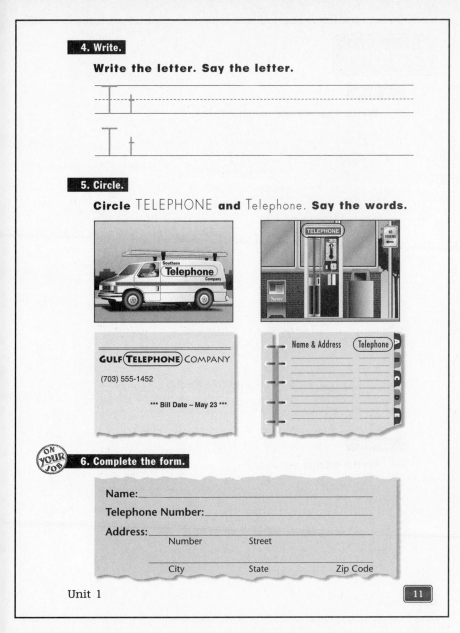

4. Write.

Write the letter. Say the letter.

5. Circle.

Circle TELEPHONE and Telephone. **Say the words.**

Southern **Telephone** Company

TELEPHONE

NO PARKING

GULF **TELEPHONE** COMPANY

(703) 555-1452

*** Bill Date – May 23 ***

Name & Address   Telephone

A B C D E

6. Complete the form.

Name:_____

Telephone Number:_____

Address:_____
          Number   Street

_____
          City   State   Zip Code

Unit 1   11

Language Note

*Teach learners to say **Hello** when answering the telephone and to say **Goodbye** at the end of the conversation.*

Environmental Print: Have learners point out examples of words with **T** and **t** they see in the room. For more information, see "Environmental Print" on page ix.

5. Help learners read the directions. Demonstrate by completing the first item on the board or overhead projector and reading the word aloud. Then have learners complete the exercise in pairs. Check each learner's work and provide feedback as needed.

6. Help learners read the directions. Demonstrate by completing the form on the board or overhead projector. Then have learners complete the activity independently. Check learners' work. Then have volunteers read aloud their names, telephone numbers, and addresses.

FOLLOW-UP

Important Telephone Numbers: Ask learners what important telephone numbers they need. Look the numbers up in the telephone book for the learners and write them on the board or overhead projector. Read the numbers aloud with the class. Have learners copy the numbers they need.

♦ Have pairs of learners exchange telephone numbers and pantomime calling each other. First, model the activity with a volunteer. Say the number you are calling aloud as you pantomime dialing on a copy of Blackline Master 10: Telephone. Prompt your partner to say *Hello.* Ask, *Is this (first name)?* Then have learners do the activity. Have learners change partners and repeat the activity.

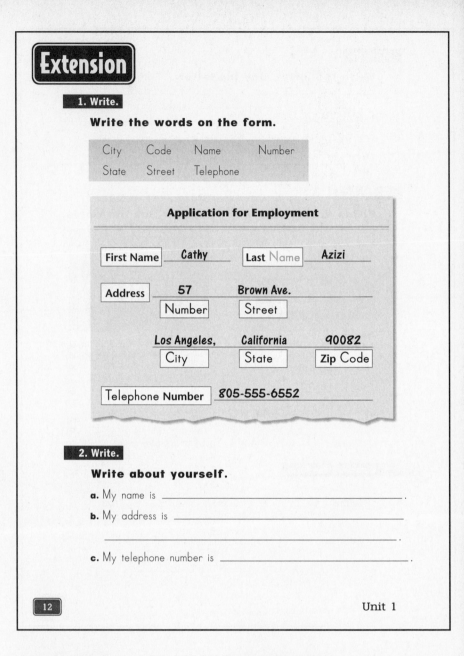

Extension

1. Write.

Write the words on the form.

City   Code   Name   Number

State   Street   Telephone

Application for Employment

First Name   **Cathy**   Last Name   **Azizi**

Address   **57**   **Brown Ave.**

          Number   Street

     Los Angeles,   **California**   **90082**

       City   State   Zip Code

Telephone Number   **805-555-6552**

2. Write.

Write about yourself.

a. My name is _____ .

b. My address is _____

_____ .

c. My telephone number is _____ .

12   Unit 1

PREPARATION

Review the new language using the following suggestions.

● Hold up word cards and/or Blackline Master 8: Identification Forms to review **first name, last name, address, number, street, city, state, zip code,** and **telephone number.** Ask volunteers to read the words and then to give the appropriate information about themselves.

● Write your name, address, and telephone number on the board or overhead projector. Hold up the word cards and have volunteers indicate the corresponding information on the board or overhead projector.

PRESENTATION

1. Focus attention on the form in the book. Help learners read the directions. Demonstrate by filling in one of the missing words on the form on the board or overhead projector. Instruct learners to fill in the missing words on the form in their books. Check learners' work.

2. Help learners read the directions. Model completing the first item on the board or overhead projector. Have learners complete the sentences about themselves. Check learners' work. Have pairs read their sentences to each other. Then have several learners read their sentences to the class.

FOLLOW-UP

Telephone Book: Have learners copy the sentences in 2 on a sheet of paper. Ask learners to draw or include a photo of themselves on the page. Compile the papers and create a class book.

♦ Have learners add their work phone numbers and addresses to the book.

Performance Check

1. Match.

1. __b__ name
2. __c__ telephone number
3. __a__ address

a. 10 Park Street

b. Ana Lee

c. 555-8819

2. Complete the form.

Application for Employment

Name: _____
      First   Last

Telephone Number: _____

Address: _____
         Number   Street

_____
City   State   Zip Code

Unit 1   13

ASAP PROJECT

Bring in some examples of identification tags such as those found on luggage or storage box labels. Then, have learners work together to create identification tags for their own personal equipment and possessions. Be sure learners include on the tags a place for name and telephone number.

PREPARATION

Briefly review the new language before learners open their books. Follow these suggestions.

● Duplicate a copy of Blackline Master 8: Identification Forms for each learner and have him or her complete it. Check learners' work carefully and provide specific help as needed until you are sure learners feel confident that they know all the new language.

PRESENTATION

Use any of the procedures in "Evaluation," page ix, with this page. Record individuals' results on the Unit 1 Individual Competency Chart. Record the class's results on the Class Cumulative Competency Chart.

INFORMAL WORKPLACE-SPECIFIC ASSESSMENT

Have learners complete the personal information section of a form that is appropriate for their companies, occupations, or career interests. Check learners' work.

Unit 2 Overview

—SCANS Competencies—

★ Acquire and evaluate information

★ Understand systems

★ Interpret and communicate information

Unit 2 Workforce Skills

● Identify places at work

● Ask for and give directions

● Ask for and find common supplies

Materials

● Letter cards for **e, l, m, r,** and **s**

● Picture cards and word cards of places at work (**office, men's room, ladies' room, exit, supply room, break room**) and supplies (**gloves, paper, notebooks, bags, envelopes,** and **towels**)

● Realia: magazines, scissors, supplies (gloves, paper, notebooks, bags, envelopes, towels), and materials associated with the various places at work (shelves, a lunch pail or thermos, files, supply order forms, and so on)

● A large floor plan of your school and/or your learners' workplace. Use the floor plan whenever referring to building layouts.

● Blackline Masters 2, 3, and 5

★　　★　　★　　★　　★

UNIT **2** **Your Workplace**

Look at the pictures.

Where are the people?

Which places can you name at work?

14

Unit 2

WORKFORCE SKILLS (page 14)

Identify places at work

★　　★　　★　　★　　★

Teaching Note

Use Blackline Masters 6 and 7: Common Directions to clarify the directions in this unit. Use page 14 to warm up learners, to draw on prior knowledge, and to spark interest.

PREPARATION

Begin the class by showing pictures of different places at work. Ask learners if they have seen these places at their work. Help them name other places they may have seen at their jobs.

PRESENTATION

Focus attention on the illustrations. Have learners say as much as they can about them. Learners may be able to name a few items in the pictures, but you may have to prompt them by naming items and having learners repeat. You might mention places at work illustrated on the page, such as the break room and supply room, and ask learners to raise their hands if they have seen them or been to them. You also might read the unit title and questions aloud and have learners answer the questions.

FOLLOW-UP

Magazine Pictures: Provide pairs of learners with magazines with pictures. Ask learners to cut out pictures of objects that they might find in or

associate with the different places illustrated on the page, such as sandwiches, coffee, and napkins with the break room. Have pairs show their pictures to the class and help them say the names of one or more of the objects in the pictures. Provide feedback as necessary.

◆ Have pairs of learners join together to make groups of four. Ask each pair to show their pictures to the other pair and name as many objects as they can for them.

Unit 2

15

Teaching Note

Use this page to introduce the new language in the unit. Whenever possible, encourage peer teaching. Supply any language the learners need.

PREPARATION

Preteach the new words in the lesson. Follow these suggestions.

● Use picture cards and word cards to teach **break room, office, supply room, men's room,** and **ladies' room.** Identify the rooms and have learners repeat. Show materials associated with each room, such as lunch pails and files. If needed, mime actions associated with the places, such as eating, typing, or washing your hands. Ask learners if they have seen these or similar places at their worksites. See "Presenting Recognition Words" on page viii.

PRESENTATION

1. Help learners read the directions. Demonstrate by completing the first item on the board or overhead projector. Have learners complete the activity in teams. Encourage learners to work together. Go over the answers with the class.

2. Help learners read the directions. Model the dialog as learners listen. Say the dialog again and have learners repeat. Ask learners to practice the dialog with a partner. Then model substituting the next place name on the page in the dialog, and ask learners to continue similarly with the remaining items.

FOLLOW-UP

Where Is It? Place the picture cards for the places in the illustrations in different parts of the room. Give volunteers the word cards. Ask the volunteers to go to the corresponding picture cards. Say, *Go to the (supply room).* Repeat with other places and other learners. Have learners remain by the picture cards.

♦ Ask volunteers, *Where is (learner's name)?* Encourage others in the class to respond with the appropriate place.

★　　★　　★　　★　　★

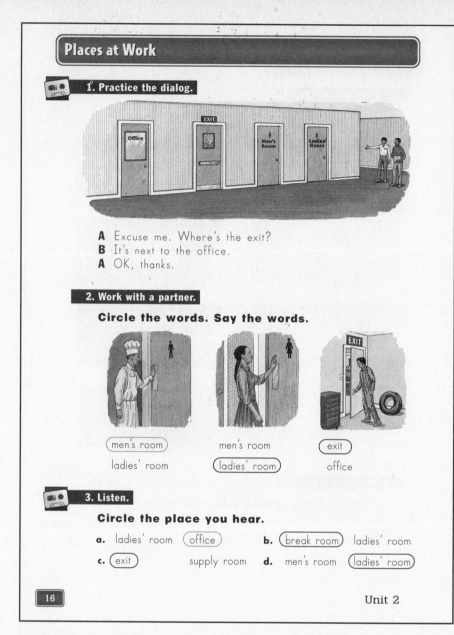

Places at Work

 1. Practice the dialog.

A Excuse me. Where's the exit?
B It's next to the office.
A OK, thanks.

2. Work with a partner.

Circle the words. Say the words.

(men's room)   men's room   (exit)
ladies' room   (ladies' room)   office

 3. Listen.

Circle the place you hear.

a. ladies' room (office)   **b.** (break room) ladies' room

c. (exit)   supply room   **d.** men's room (ladies' room)

16

Unit 2

Language Note

Learners may hear men's and ladies' rooms called by different names. You might present a few common alternatives: **rest room, women's room, bathroom,** *etc.*

PREPARATION

Preteach or review the new language in the lesson. Follow these suggestions.

● Use picture cards and word cards to preteach or review **exit, office, men's room, ladies' room, break room,** and **supply room.** Follow the instructions on page 15. See also "Presenting Recognition Words" on page viii.

● Preteach the dialog. If necessary, introduce or review the phrase **next to.** Place picture cards for the office and exit adjacent to each other. Pantomime looking for a place. Ask, *Where's the exit?* Model the question and have learners repeat. Then model the answer, *It's next to the office.* Have learners repeat.

PRESENTATION

1. Focus attention on the illustration. Help learners identify rooms and read the signs. Have them say as much as they can about the illustration. You may want to cue them by indicating the items and having learners say the names, or by saying names of items and having learners indicate them. Restate learners' ideas in acceptable English and write them on the board or overhead projector.

Present the dialog. See "Presenting Dialogs" on page viii.

2. Help learners read the directions. Demonstrate by completing the first item on the board or overhead projector and then reading the words aloud. Then have learners complete the exercise in

pairs. Check the exercise on the board or overhead projector.

3. Help learners read the directions. Then present the listening activity. See "Presenting Listening Activities" on page ix. Check learners' work. Ask volunteers to read their answers aloud.

4. Present or review the letters **e** and **m.** See "Presenting Letters" on page ix. Then have learners complete the exercise. Check learners' work. For extra reinforcement, use Blackline Master 2: Alphabet A-M and Blackline Master 5: Lined Paper.

Environmental Print: Have learners point out examples of words with the letters **E, e, M,** and **m** they see in the room. For more information, see "Environmental Print" on page ix.

4. Write.

Write the letters. Say the letters. Say the words.

E e

E e

M m

M m

_E_xit   _e_xit   _M_en's Roo_m_   _m_en's roo_m_

____xit   ____xit   ____en's Roo____   ____en's roo____

____xit   ____xit   ____en's Roo____   ____en's roo____

5. Match.

Look at the picture in 1. Write the letter.

1. A Where's the men's room?   **a.** men's room

   B It's next to the __c__.

2. A Where's the exit?   **b.** exit

   B It's next to the __a__.

3. A Where's the office?   **c.** ladies' room

   B It's next to the __b__.

6. Work with a partner.

Practice the dialogs in 5.

Unit 2   17

---

5. Help learners read the directions. Demonstrate by completing the first item on the board or overhead projector. Then ask learners to complete the exercise independently. Check learners' work. Then ask volunteers to read their answers aloud.

6. Help learners read the directions. Demonstrate with a volunteer. Then have learners complete the activity in pairs, switching partners and repeating the activity several times. Invite several pairs to present the dialogs to the class.

FOLLOW-UP

Giving Directions: Show the large building map or floor plan. Have pairs use the dialog on the page to ask and answer questions about the location of the places on the building map or floor plan.

♦ Have volunteers come forward to ask the class for the locations of places on the building map. As learners answer, have the volunteer find the place and point to it.

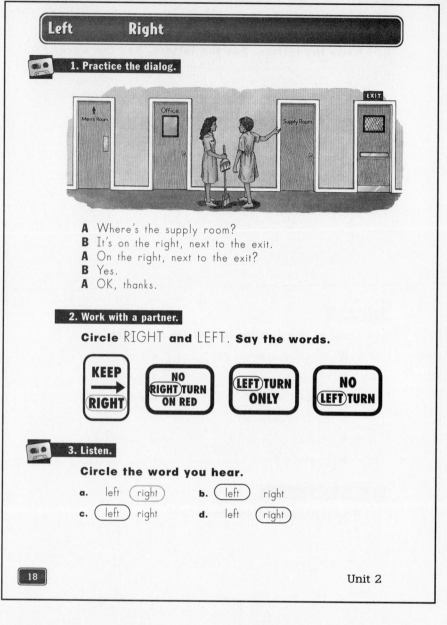

Left   Right

 1. Practice the dialog.

A Where's the supply room?
B It's on the right, next to the exit.
A On the right, next to the exit?
B Yes.
A OK, thanks.

2. Work with a partner.

Circle RIGHT and LEFT. Say the words.

KEEP → RIGHT   NO RIGHT TURN ON RED   LEFT TURN ONLY   NO LEFT TURN

 3. Listen.

Circle the word you hear.

a. left (right)   b. (left) right

c. (left) right   d. left (right)

18   Unit 2

PREPARATION

Preteach the new language in the lesson. Follow these suggestions.

● Use gestures and word cards to preteach the recognition words **left** and **right.** Stand in the front of the class facing the same direction as the learners. Point to the left and say *Left.* Point to the right and say *Right.* Refer to people and things in the room to convey the meanings and to practice the direction words. See "Presenting Recognition Words" on page viii.

● Preteach the dialog. Arrange some of the workplace picture cards on the left side of the room and the others on the right side. Ask volunteers to tell you where the places are. Model the question, *Where's the (break room)?* Have

learners repeat. Then model the answer, *It's on the (left), next to (the exit).* Have learners repeat.

PRESENTATION

1. Focus attention on the illustration. Help learners identify the places in the building and read the labels on the rooms. Have them say as much as they can about the illustration. You may want to cue them by indicating the items and having learners say the names or by saying names of items and having learners indicate them. Restate their ideas in acceptable English and write them on the board or overhead projector.

Present the dialog. See "Presenting Dialogs" on page viii.

2. Help learners read the directions. Demonstrate by completing the first item on the board or overhead projector. Then have them complete the exercise in pairs. Check the exercise on the board or overhead projector.

3. Help learners read the directions. Then present the listening activity. See "Presenting Listening Activities" on page ix. Check learners' work. Ask volunteers to read their answers aloud.

4. Present or review the letters **l** and **r.** See "Presenting Letters" on page ix. Then have learners complete the exercise. Check learners' work. For extra reinforcement, use Blackline Masters 2 and 3: Alphabet and Blackline Master 5: Lined Paper.

4. Write.

Write the letters. Say the letters. Say the words.

L

Ll

Rr

Rr

__L__adies' __R__oom ____adies' ____oom ____adies' ____oom

__l__eft ____eft ____eft __r__ight ____ight ____ight

supp__l__y __r__oom supp____y ____oom supp____y ____oom

5. Circle.

Look at the picture in I. Circle left or right.

1. A Where's the supply room?

  B It's on the   left.   (right.)

2. A Where's the men's room?

  B It's on the   (left.)   right.

3. A Where's the office?

  B It's on the   (left.)   right.

6. Work with a partner.

Practice the dialogs in 5.

Unit 2   19

Environmental Print: Have learners point out examples of words with the letters **L, l, R,** and **r** they see in the room. For more information, see "Environmental Print" on page ix.

5. Help learners read the directions. Demonstrate by completing the first item on the board or overhead projector. Then ask learners to complete the exercise independently. Check learners' work. Then ask volunteers to read the answers aloud.

6. Help learners read the directions. Demonstrate the activity with a volunteer. Then have learners complete the activity. Invite pairs to present the dialogs to the class.

FOLLOW-UP

A New Worker: Play the role of a new worker coming to the building for the first time. Ask the location of some place in the building and have a volunteer provide an answer. Repeat several times, asking questions about a different place each time. Supply any language learners need.

♦ Allow learners to practice the role play in pairs. Have learners switch roles and repeat the activity.

WORKFORCE SKILLS (pages 20-21)

Ask for and find common supplies

Ask for and give directions

★   ★   ★   ★   ★

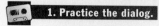

Supply Room

 1. Practice the dialog.

A I need paper.
B Paper's in the supply room.
A Where's the supply room?
B It's on the right.

2. Work with a partner.

Say the words.

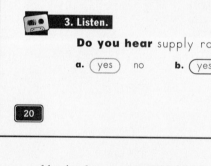

bags · towels · paper · notebooks · envelopes · gloves

 3. Listen.

Do you hear supply room? **Circle** yes **or** no.

a. (yes)   no   **b.** (yes)   no   **c.** yes   (no)

20   Unit 2

Language Note

If learners ask, explain that **supplies** *means more than one supply.*

PREPARATION

Preteach the new language in the lesson. Follow these suggestions.

● Use picture cards, word cards, and real items to preteach the words **supply room, paper, gloves, bags, envelopes, towels,** and **notebooks.** See "Presenting Recognition Words" on page viii.

● Preteach the dialog. Model the statement, *I need paper.* Have learners repeat. Then model the response, *Paper's in the supply room.* Have learners repeat.

PRESENTATION

 1. Focus attention on the illustration. Have learners say as much as they can about it. You may wish to cue them by indicating the

items and having learners say the names, or by saying names of items and having learners point them out. Restate their ideas in acceptable English and write them on the board or overhead projector.

Present the dialog. See "Presenting Dialogs" on page viii.

2. Help learners read the directions. Demonstrate by indicating the paper in the picture and saying the word **paper.** Then have learners complete the exercise in pairs. Have volunteers say the words aloud to the class.

3. Help learners read the directions. Then present the listening activity. See "Presenting Listening Activities" on page ix. Check learners' work. Ask volunteers to read their answers aloud.

4. Present or review the letter **s.** See "Presenting Letters" on page ix. Then have learners complete the exercise. Check learners' work. For additional reinforcement, use Blackline Master 3: Alphabet N-Z and Blackline Master 5: Lined Paper.

Environmental Print: Have learners point out examples of words with **S** and **s** they see in the room. For more information, see "Environmental Print" on page ix.

4. Write.

Write the letter. Say the letter. Say the words.

$S\ s$

$S\ s$

__s__upply ____upply ____upply ____upply ____upply

 ON YOUR JOB

5. Check.

Check the supplies you use.
Read the items to a partner.

Supplies

Name: _____

1. gloves _____   2. paper ✓
3. envelopes _____   4. bags _____
5. notebooks _____   6. towels _____

6. Match.

What supplies do the people use?
Look at 5. Write the number of the supply.

a. __4__   b. __2__   c. __1__

Unit 2   `21`

ON YOUR JOB **5.** Help learners read the directions. Demonstrate by checking supply items you use on the board or overhead projector. Then have learners complete the exercise independently. Check learners' work. Have learners read their lists in pairs. Then ask volunteers to read their lists to the class.

6. Focus attention on the illustrations. Have learners describe the workers in as much detail as they can. Then help learners read the directions. Demonstrate by filling in the number of the appropriate supply in the first item on the board or overhead projector. Have learners complete the activity in pairs. Check learners' work.

FOLLOW-UP

I Need Paper: Arrange learners in small groups. Provide each group with pictures of supplies and/or real supplies. Have each learner in the group, in turn, identify some supply that he or she needs by saying *(Learner's name), I need paper.* The person named should find and give the correct supply to the first person. Finally, have each learner hold up the item he or she needed and name it for the class.

♦ Have each group write a list of supplies that its members asked for. Ask each group to choose a volunteer to read the group's list to the class.

WORKFORCE SKILLS (pages 22-23)

Ask for and find common supplies

Ask for and give directions

★ ★ ★ ★ ★

SCANS Note

You may want to point out that returning reusable supplies and equipment back to their proper places is an effective way to keep track of and maintain resources.

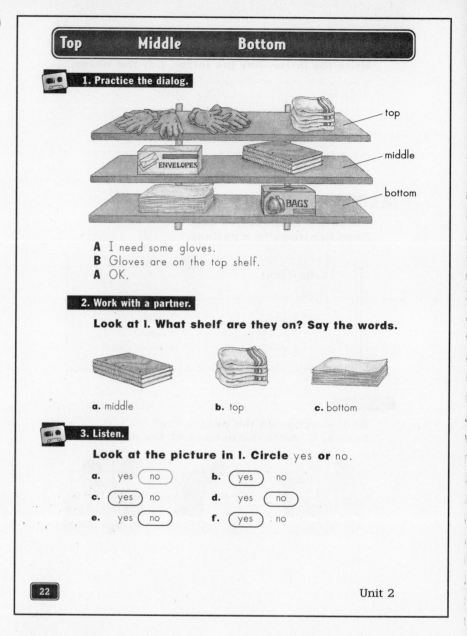

Top   Middle   Bottom

1. Practice the dialog.

top

middle

bottom

ENVELOPES

BAGS

A I need some gloves.
B Gloves are on the top shelf.
A OK.

2. Work with a partner.

Look at 1. What shelf are they on? Say the words.

a. middle   **b.** top   **c.** bottom

3. Listen.

Look at the picture in 1. Circle yes **or** no.

a. yes (no)   **b.** (yes) no

c. (yes) no   **d.** yes (no)

e. yes (no)   **f.** (yes) no

Unit 2

PREPARATION

Preteach the new language in the lesson. Follow these suggestions.

• Use picture cards, real supplies, and word cards to review the names of supplies: **paper, notebooks, gloves, towels, envelopes,** and **bags.**

• Preteach the dialog. Use a picture of shelves, real shelves, or the illustration on this page to preteach the words **top, middle,** and **bottom.** Identify the shelves and have learners repeat. Say, *I need some gloves.* Have learners repeat. Then model the answer, *Gloves are on the top shelf.* Continue similarly with the other supplies and shelves in the illustration.

PRESENTATION

1. Focus attention on the illustration. Have learners say as much as they can about the illustration. You may want to cue them by indicating the items and having learners say the names, or by saying names of items and having learners point them out. Restate their ideas in acceptable English and write them on the board or overhead projector.

Present the dialog. See "Presenting Dialogs" on page viii.

2. Help learners read the directions. Demonstrate by indicating the first picture and saying the word **middle.** Then point to the notebooks in the

picture in number 1 and repeat the word **middle.** Repeat the procedure for the towels and paper. Then have learners complete the exercise in pairs. Have volunteers read the words aloud to the class.

3. Help learners read the directions. Then present the listening activity. See "Presenting Listening Activities" on page ix.

4. Help learners read the directions. Demonstrate by completing the first item on the board or overhead projector. Then have learners write the letters independently and say the words in pairs. Ask volunteers to say the words aloud.

4. Write.

Write the letters. Say the words.

pape _r_   pape ____   pape ____

_m_ iddl _e_   ____ iddl ____   ____ iddl ____

towe _l_ _s_   towe ____ ____   towe ____ ____

5. Match.

Where are the supplies? Answer the questions.

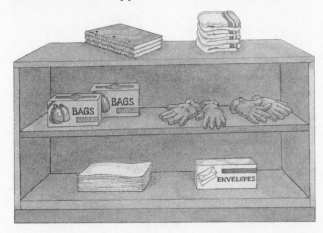

_c_ **1.** Where are the notebooks?   **a.** On the bottom shelf

_a_ **2.** Where is the paper?   **b.** On the middle shelf

_b_ **3.** Where are the bags?   **c.** On the top shelf

6. Work with a partner.

Practice the dialogs in 5.

Unit 2

23

Culture Note

*Tell learners they should say **Thanks** or **Thank you** after getting information or help.*

5. Help learners read the directions. Demonstrate by completing the first item on the board or overhead projector. Then ask learners to complete the exercise independently. Check learners' work. Then ask volunteers to read the answers aloud.

6. Help learners read the directions. Demonstrate practicing the dialogs with a volunteer. Then have learners work with partners to practice. Invite pairs to present the dialogs to the class.

FOLLOW-UP

Making Labels: Have learners make labels that say **top, middle,** and **bottom.** Help learners place the labels correctly in various places or on objects in the room, such as on the top of a desk, in the middle of the chalkboard, on the bottom drawer of a file cabinet, and so on.

♦ Give a series of commands for learners to follow that refer to the labeled places in the room. For example, say, *Put the paper in the bottom drawer* or *Put the books on the top shelf.* Model language for labeled items that learners may not know, such as **drawer.** You may want to give the commands first and demonstrate the actions yourself. Then ask volunteers to perform the actions.

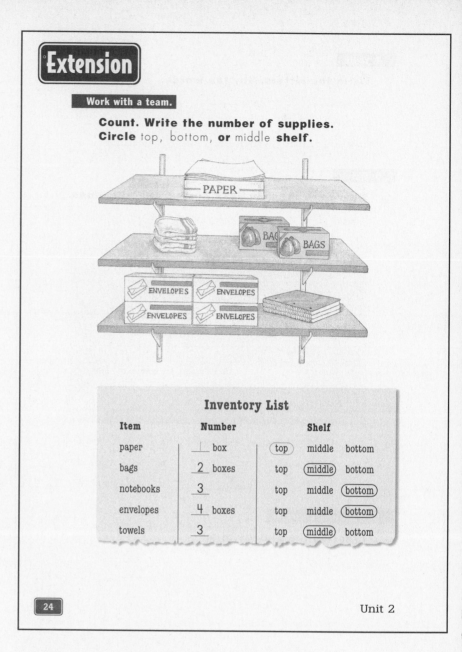

Extension

Work with a team.

Count. Write the number of supplies.
Circle top, bottom, **or** middle **shelf.**

PAPER

BAGS BAGS

ENVELOPES ENVELOPES
ENVELOPES ENVELOPES

Inventory List

Item	Number		Shelf	
paper	_1_ box	(top)	middle	bottom
bags	_2_ boxes	top	(middle)	bottom
notebooks	_3_	top	middle	(bottom)
envelopes	_4_ boxes	top	middle	(bottom)
towels	_3_	top	(middle)	bottom

24

Unit 2

PREPARATION

Review the new language using the following suggestions.

● Hold up word cards for **gloves, note-books, envelopes, towels, paper,** and **bags.** Ask volunteers to read the words and then to point to the corresponding pictures or supplies.

PRESENTATION

Focus attention on the supply shelves. Ask learners to say as much as they can about them. Restate learners' ideas in acceptable English and write them on the board or overhead projector. If needed, help learners count the supplies and identify the shelves where the supplies are located.

Then help learners read the directions. Demonstrate the activity on the board or overhead projector by filling in the number of boxes of paper and circling the shelf where it is located.

Arrange learners in teams to complete the activity. Ask several volunteers to say their answers for you to write on the board or overhead projector.

FOLLOW-UP

Have learners work in teams to create an inventory list for objects found in one part of the room. Learners can list the names, number, and locations of the items they find.

♦ Ask for items on the inventory list and have learners retrieve the items.

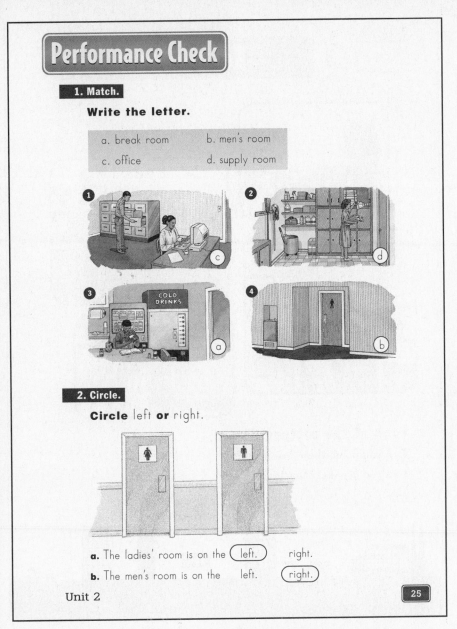

Performance Check

1. Match.

Write the letter.

a. break room	b. men's room
c. office	d. supply room

2. Circle.

Circle left or right.

a. The ladies' room is on the (left.) right.

b. The men's room is on the left. (right.)

Unit 2 `25`

ASAP PROJECT

Take your learners on a tour of the building. Pause at various rooms to identify room names, people in rooms, and purposes of rooms. After you return to the classroom, help learners draw a floor plan of the building on a large sheet of paper. Tell them to mark important places, such as rest rooms, exits, the break room, and so on.

Ask learners in pairs to describe the building to each other. Instruct them to say as much about it as they can. Have several volunteers describe the building aloud to the class. Learners can later use the building floor plan to help orient new learners or workers.

PREPARATION

Briefly review the new language before learners open their books. Follow these suggestions.

● Write the words in the activities on the board or overhead projector and ask volunteers to find the matching picture cards.

Provide specific help as needed until you are sure learners are confident that they know all the new language.

PRESENTATION

Use any of the procedures in "Evaluation," page ix, with this page. Record individuals' results on the Unit 2 Individual Competency Chart. Record the class's results on the Class Cumulative Competency Chart.

INFORMAL WORKPLACE-SPECIFIC ASSESSMENT

Have learners name one or two supplies and one or two places at their jobs.

Unit 3 Overview

—SCANS Competencies—

★ Select technology
★ Apply technology to tasks
★ Teach others

Unit 3 Workforce Skills

* Identify common machines
* Give and follow instructions to use a machine
* Read simple instructions

Materials

* Letter cards for **p, o, s,** and **u**
* Picture cards and word cards of machines in the unit (**vacuum cleaner, dishwasher, copier, coffee maker, dryer, microwave oven,** and **washing machine**) and a picture of a machine control panel with several colored buttons, including a green one
* Pictures or photographs of machines from learners' workplaces
* Word cards for **push, pull, on, off, start, stop, put in, take out, open,** and **close**
* Word cards and realia or picture cards for other items that can be opened and closed: envelope, bag, notebook
* Blackline Masters 3 and 5

UNIT **3** **Technology**

Look at the pictures.

Can you name these machines?
Can you use these machines?

26

Unit 3

WORKFORCE SKILLS (page 26)

Identify common machines

Teaching Note

Use Blackline Masters 6 and 7: Common Directions to clarify the directions in this unit. Use page 26 to warm up learners, to draw on prior knowledge, and to spark interest.

PREPARATION

Show pictures of different machines at work. Encourage learners to identify machines that they know or can use. Talk about where the machines might be located at work. Model names of machines as needed and have learners repeat.

PRESENTATION

Focus attention on the illustrations. Have learners say as much as they can about them. Learners may be able to name a few items in the pictures, but you may have to prompt them by naming items and having learners repeat. You also might read the unit title and questions aloud and have learners answer the questions. Model any words learners do not know.

FOLLOW-UP

What's at Work? Take learners for a walk around the building. Elicit names learners may already know for machines. Model any words learners want to know. When you return to the classroom, ask, *What machines do you use?* and write the items learners name on the board or overhead projector.

♦ Have learners look around the classroom and name as many forms of technology as they can (such as the overhead projector, intercom, and lights). Model any words learners want to know. Write the words on the board or overhead projector.

Identify common machines

★　　★　　★　　★　　★

Getting Started

1. Work with a team.

Name the machines. Circle on or off.

a vacuum cleaner
(on)　off

b dishwasher
on　(off)

c copier
on　(off)

d coffee maker
(on)　off

e dryer
on　(off)

f microwave oven
(on)　off

2. Work with a partner.

Point to the pictures. Ask your partner questions.

A Is the vacuum cleaner on?
B Yes.

Unit 3

27

Teaching Note

Use this page to introduce the new language in the unit. Whenever possible, encourage peer teaching. Supply any language the learners need.

PREPARATION

Preteach the new words in the lesson. Follow these suggestions. See also "Presenting Recognition Words" on page viii.

● Display picture cards and word cards for the machines on the page: **vacuum cleaner, dishwasher, copier, coffee maker, dryer,** and **microwave oven.** Encourage learners to talk about the machines, what they are used for, where they are located, and who uses them. Allow learners to comment on other machines at their workplaces.

● To teach **on** and **off,** point to the room's light switch. Turn the light on and off. Model the words and have learners repeat. Hold up the word cards for **on** and **off** and ask, *Is the light (on)?* Have learners repeat the target word.

PRESENTATION

1. Help learners read the directions. Demonstrate by completing the first item on the board or overhead projector. Have learners complete the exercise in teams. Encourage learners to work together. Check the answers with the class.

2. Help learners read the directions. Model the dialog as learners listen. Say the dialog again and have learners repeat. Ask learners to practice the dialog with a partner. Then model substituting the next item on the page in the dialog, and ask learners to continue similarly with the remaining items.

FOLLOW-UP

Workplace Technology: Bring in photographs or pictures of machines from learners' workplaces. Help learners identify the machines and identify, if possible, if they are on or off. Allow learners to share information and experiences they have had with the various machines.

◆ Display the pictures or photos of the machines. Say, *Point to the (name of machine).* Have learners point to the appropriate picture. Then ask, *Is it on or off?* Learners can respond according to the photo or picture.

WORKFORCE SKILLS (pages 28-29)

Give and follow instructions to use a machine

★   ★   ★   ★   ★

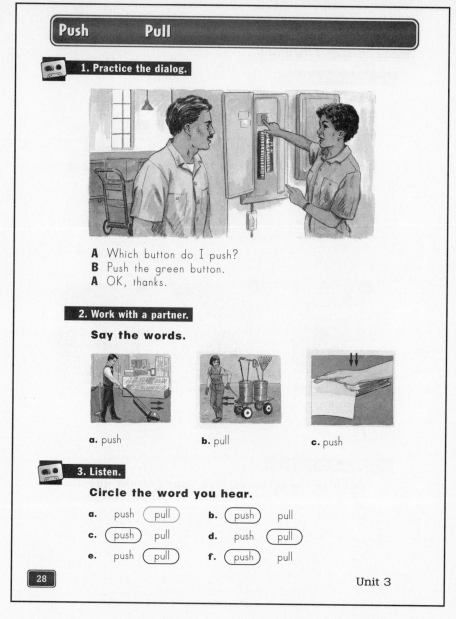

Push   Pull

1. Practice the dialog.

A Which button do I push?
B Push the green button.
A OK, thanks.

2. Work with a partner.

Say the words.

a. push   **b.** pull   **c.** push

 3. Listen.

Circle the word you hear.

a. push (pull)   **b.** (push) pull
c. (push) pull   **d.** push (pull)
e. push (pull)   **f.** (push) pull

28   Unit 3

Language Note

*Point out that in the word **telephone** the letters **ph** represent the sound /f/.*

PREPARATION

Preteach the new language in the lesson. Follow these suggestions.

● Use word cards, picture cards, and pantomime to preteach the recognition words **push** and **pull**. See "Presenting Recognition Words" on page viii.

● Preteach the dialog. If necessary, introduce or review the question **Which button do I push?** Draw or show a picture of a machine control panel with several colored buttons (including a green one). Pantomime trying to decide which button to push. Ask, *Which button do I push?* Model the question and have learners repeat.

Then demonstrate pushing the green button and model the answer, *Push the green button.* Have learners repeat. If necessary, use objects in the room to clarify the colors red and green.

PRESENTATION

 1. Focus attention on the illustration. Help learners identify the place. Have them say as much as they can about the illustration. You may want to cue them by indicating the items and having learners say the names, or by saying names of items and having learners indicate them. Restate learners' ideas in acceptable English and write them on the board or overhead projector. Then present the dialog. See "Presenting Dialogs" on page viii.

2. Help learners read the directions. Demonstrate the first item by reading the word aloud. Then have learners complete the exercise in pairs.

3. Help learners read the directions. Then present the listening activity. See "Presenting Listening Activities" on page ix. Check learners' work. Ask volunteers to read their answers aloud.

4. Present or review the letter **p.** See "Presenting Letters" on page ix. Then have learners complete the exercise. Check learners' work. For extra reinforcement, use Blackline Master 3: Alphabet N-Z and Blackline Master 5: Lined Paper.

Environmental Print: Have learners point out examples of words with **P** and **p** they see in the room. For more

28

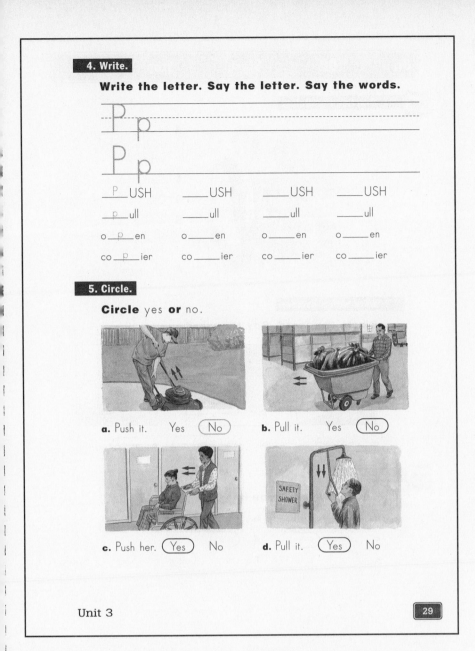

4. Write.

Write the letter. Say the letter. Say the words.

P p

P p

P_USH   ___USH   ___USH   ___USH
p_ull   ___ull   ___ull   ___ull
o_p_en   o___en   o___en   o___en
co_p_ier co___ier co___ier co___ier

5. Circle.

Circle yes **or** no.

a. Push it.   Yes   (No)

b. Pull it.   Yes   (No)

c. Push her.   (Yes)   No

d. Pull it.   (Yes)   No

Unit 3   29

---

information, see "Environmental Print" on page ix.

5. Help learners read the directions. Demonstrate by completing the first item on the board or overhead projector. Then ask learners to complete the exercise independently. Check learners' work. Then ask volunteers to read the answers aloud.

FOLLOW-UP

Following Instructions: Give a series of commands for learners to follow. For example: *Push open the door. Pull down the shade. Push the table. Pull the chair.* First, give the command and demonstrate the action yourself. Then give the command without visual cues and have a learner carry it out.

♦ Give learners copies of word cards with **push** and **pull.** Ask learners to place the word cards at appropriate places in the room where the instruction words apply. For example: on the door, on a file cabinet, on a window shade.

WORKFORCE SKILLS (pages 30-31)

Give and follow instructions to use a machine

★   ★   ★   ★   ★

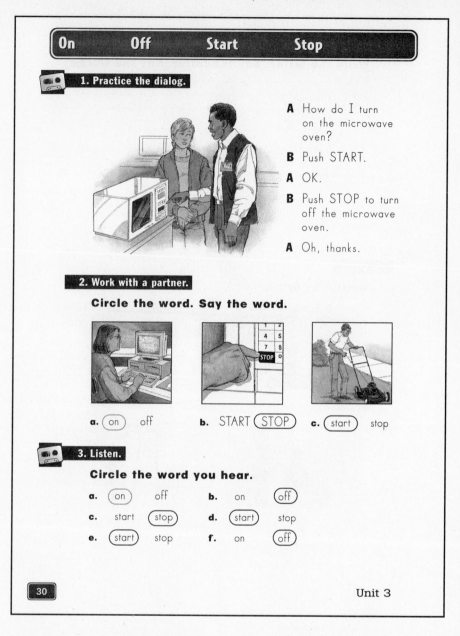

Language Note

Not all machines use the same words for the same functions. For example, **on** *and* **start** *are synonyms for making the machine operate;* **off** *and* **stop** *are used to indicate ceasing operation of the machine. For some more complex machines, there may be two steps, such as turning on the machine (starting the machine motor) and then starting the machine or putting the machine in motion.*

PREPARATION

Preteach the new language in the lesson. Follow these suggestions.

● Preteach or review the words **on, off, start,** and **stop.** Follow the procedure on page 27 to teach **on** and **off.** To teach **start** and **stop,** use an audiocassette player. Start the player, hold up the word card for **start,** and say, *Start.* Then stop the player, hold up the word card for **stop,** and say, *Stop.* Have learners repeat the words. See "Presenting Recognition Words" on page viii.

● Preteach the dialog. Display a machine or picture of a machine and say, *How do I turn on the (name of machine)?* Have learners repeat. Draw buttons labeled START and STOP on the board. Then model the answer,

Push START and demonstrate pushing the START button you drew. Have learners repeat. Ask, *How do I turn off the (name of machine)?* Model the answer, *Push STOP to turn off the (name of machine)* and demonstrate pushing the STOP button you drew. Have learners repeat the answer.

PRESENTATION

1. Focus attention on the illustration. Help learners identify the place and the machine. Have them say as much as they can about the illustration. You may want to cue them by indicating the items and having learners say the names, or by saying the names of items and having learners indicate them. Restate their ideas in acceptable English and write them on the board or overhead projector.

Present the dialog. See "Presenting Dialogs" on page viii.

2. Help learners read the directions. Demonstrate by completing the first item on the board or overhead projector. Then have learners complete the exercise in pairs. Check the exercise on the board or overhead projector. Have volunteers read the answers aloud.

3. Help learners read the directions. Then present the listening activity. See "Presenting Listening Activities" on page ix. Check learners' work. Ask volunteers to read their answers aloud.

4. Present or review the letters **o** and **s.** See "Presenting Letters" on page ix. Then have learners complete the exercise. Check learners' work. For extra

4. Write.

Write the letters. Say the letters. Say the words.

O o

O o

S s

S s

O FF	___ FF	___ FF	___ FF
o pen	___ pen	___ pen	___ pen
S TART	___ TART	___ TART	___ TART
s top	___ top	___ top	___ top

5. Write.

Complete the dialogs. Write STOP or START.

A How do I turn on the coffee maker?

B Push _____ START _____ .

A How do I turn off the microwave oven?

B Push _____ STOP _____ .

6. Work with a partner.

Practice the dialogs in 5.

Unit 3

31

SCANS Note

Tell learners to make sure they know how to turn off a new or unfamiliar machine before they start to use it.

Language Note

*Point out that the letters **sh,** as in **push,** can represent the sound /sh/.*

reinforcement, use Blackline Master 3: Alphabet N-Z and Blackline Master 5: Lined Paper.

Environmental Print: Have learners point out examples of words with the letters **O, o, S,** and **s** they see in the room. For more information, see "Environmental Print" on page ix.

5. Help learners read the directions. Demonstrate by completing the first item on the board or overhead projector. Then ask learners to complete the exercise independently. Check learners' work.

6. Help learners read the directions. Demonstrate saying the dialogs with a volunteer. Then have learners work with partners to practice. Invite pairs to present the dialogs to the class.

FOLLOW-UP

Buttons and Switches: Have pairs of learners brainstorm names of machines that have **on, off, start,** and/or **stop** buttons or switches. Have pairs share their lists with the class.

♦ Have pairs of learners write dialogs about how to use the machines on their lists. For example, *How do I turn on the washing machine? Push ON.* Have pairs present their dialogs to the class.

WORKFORCE SKILLS (pages 32-33)

Give and follow instructions to use a machine

Read simple instructions

★   ★   ★   ★   ★

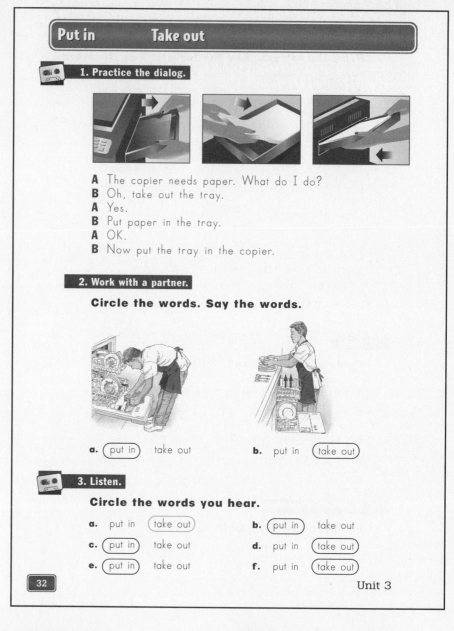

Put in   Take out

1. Practice the dialog.

A The copier needs paper. What do I do?
B Oh, take out the tray.
A Yes.
B Put paper in the tray.
A OK.
B Now put the tray in the copier.

2. Work with a partner.

Circle the words. Say the words.

a. (put in)   take out   b. put in   (take out)

3. Listen.

Circle the words you hear.

a. put in (take out)   b. (put in) take out
c. (put in) take out   d. put in (take out)
e. (put in) take out   f. put in (take out)

32   Unit 3

PREPARATION

Preteach the new language in the lesson. Follow these suggestions.

• Use picture cards, word cards, and pantomime to teach the phrases **put in** and **take out.** See "Presenting Recognition Words" on page viii.

• Preteach the dialog. Show learners a real copier, a picture of a copier, or the illustration on the Student Book page. Then show a real paper tray that's empty and paper, or show the illustration in the book. Model the statement and question, *The copier needs paper. What do I do?* Have learners repeat. Then demonstrate and say the steps one at a time: *Take out the tray. Put paper in the tray. Put the tray in the copier.* Have learners repeat.

PRESENTATION

 1. Focus attention on the illustration. Have learners say as much as they can about it. You may wish to cue them by indicating the items for learners to say, or by saying names of items and having learners indicate them. Restate their ideas in acceptable English and write them on the board or overhead projector.

Present the dialog. See "Presenting Dialogs" on page viii.

2. Help learners read the directions. Demonstrate by completing the first item on the board or overhead projector. Then have learners complete the exercise in pairs. Check learners' work. Ask volunteers to read the answers to the class.

 3. Help learners read the directions. Then present the listening activity. See "Presenting Listening Activities" on page ix. Check learners' work. Ask volunteers to read their answers aloud.

4. Help learners read the directions. Demonstrate by completing the first item on the board or overhead projector. Then ask learners to complete the exercise independently. Check learners' work.

5. Focus attention on the illustrations. Help learners identify the machine, the other items, and the actions in as much detail as they can. Then help learners read the directions. Demonstrate by completing the first item on the board or overhead projector. Have learners

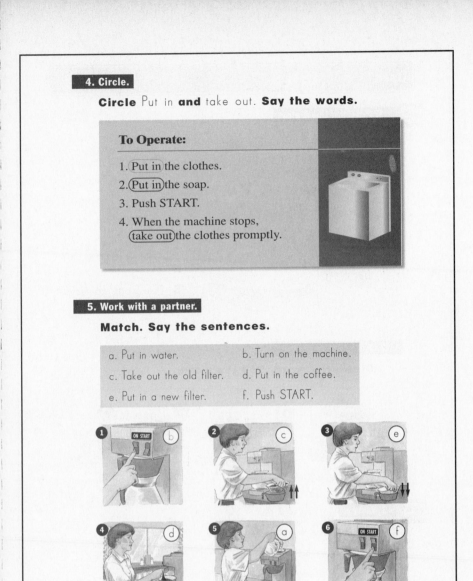

4. Circle.

Circle Put in **and** take out. **Say the words.**

To Operate:

1. (Put in) the clothes.
2. (Put in) the soap.
3. Push START.
4. When the machine stops,
   (take out) the clothes promptly.

5. Work with a partner.

Match. Say the sentences.

a. Put in water.
b. Turn on the machine.
c. Take out the old filter.
d. Put in the coffee.
e. Put in a new filter.
f. Push START.

Unit 3

33

---

complete the activity in pairs. Check learners' work. Then ask volunteers to say the answers aloud.

FOLLOW-UP

Scrambled Instructions: Arrange learners in small groups. Provide each group with the instructions from activity 5 on separate strips of paper. Ask learners to circle the recognition words on the instructions: **put in, take out, on, push,** and **start.** Have the groups arrange the strips of paper in the correct order. Finally, ask volunteers to read the sentences aloud in the proper order.

♦ Have learners role-play asking for and giving instructions using the strips. Model asking for help with a volunteer: *How do I make coffee?* Have the volunteer give the instructions. Allow learners to practice their role plays in pairs and then invite them to present their conversations to the class. As they give their presentations, other learners should scramble and reorder their strips.

WORKFORCE SKILLS (pages 34-35)

Give and follow instructions to use a
 machine

Read simple instructions

★   ★   ★   ★   ★

SCANS Note

*Emphasize that learners should always
ask someone for help if they do not
know how to use a machine or tool
at their workplace. Proper use of a
machine or tool is important not only
for the machine's/tool's maintenance,
but also for safety reasons.*

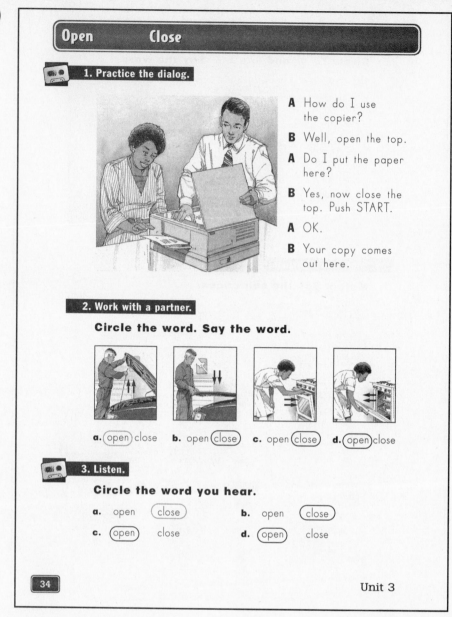

Open   Close

 1. Practice the dialog.

A How do I use
the copier?

B Well, open the top.

A Do I put the paper
here?

B Yes, now close the
top. Push START.

A OK.

B Your copy comes
out here.

2. Work with a partner.

Circle the word. Say the word.

a. (open) close   **b.** open (close)   **c.** open (close)   **d.** (open) close

 3. Listen.

Circle the word you hear.

a. open (close)   **b.** open (close)

c. (open) close   **d.** (open) close

34   Unit 3

PREPARATION

Preteach the new language in the lesson.
Follow these suggestions.

● Use picture cards, word cards, and
pantomime to teach the recognition
words **open** and **close.** Demonstrate and
have learners demonstrate opening and
closing envelopes, bags, notebooks,
books, doors, windows, and other
objects in the room. See "Presenting
Recognition Words" on page viii.

● Preteach the dialog. Ask, *How do I
use the copier?* Look puzzled. Then
have learners watch or demonstrate
making a copy on a copier in the building. Alternatively, use a picture of a
copier or the illustration on this page
to preteach the steps and introduce the
word **top.** Ask again, *How do I use the
copier?* Have learners repeat. Then

model the first step and have learners
repeat. Continue similarly with the
other steps.

PRESENTATION

1. Focus attention on the
illustration. Have learners say
as much as they can about it.
You may want to cue them by indicating the items for learners to say, or by
saying names of items and having learners indicate them. Restate their ideas in
acceptable English and write them on
the board or overhead projector.

Present the dialog. See "Presenting
Dialogs" on page viii.

2. Help learners read the directions.
Demonstrate by completing the first
item on the board or overhead projector.

Then have them complete the exercise
in pairs. Check learners' work. Have
volunteers read the answers aloud.

3. Help learners read the
directions. Then present
the listening activity. See
"Presenting Listening Activities" on
page ix. Ask volunteers to read the
correct answers aloud.

4. Present or review the letter **u.** See
"Presenting Letters" on page ix. Then
have learners complete the exercise.
Check learners' work. For extra rein-
forcement, use Blackline Master 3:
Alphabet N-Z and Blackline Master 5:
Lined Paper.

Environmental Print: Have learners
point out examples of words with **U**
and **u** they see in the room. For more

4. Write.

Write the letter. Say the letter. Say the words.

U̲ u

U u

vac_u_ _u_m vac___ ___m vac___ ___m vac___ ___m

p_u_sh p___sh p___sh p___sh

p_u_ll p___ll p___ll p___ll

o_u_t o___t o___t o___t

5. Circle.

Circle OPEN and CLOSE. Say the words.

DANGER

DO
NOT
OPEN

PLEASE
CLOSE
THE DOOR

CAUTION
THESE DOORS
CLOSE
AUTOMATICALLY

CAUTION
OPEN DOOR
SLOWLY!

Unit 3

35

---

information, see "Environmental Print" on page ix.

5. Help learners read the directions. Demonstrate by completing the first item on the board or overhead projector. Then have learners complete the exercise independently. Check learners' work. Then ask volunteers to say the words aloud.

FOLLOW-UP

Classroom Search: Ask teams of learners to find five things in the room that they can open, close, push, or pull. Invite a volunteer from each team to demonstrate the actions with the things they found and to say the appropriate action word for each.

♦ Have pairs of learners take turns giving each other commands to push, pull, open, and close the things they found as well as other objects in the room. Then have learners change partners and repeat the activity. Ask several pairs to demonstrate the activity to the class.

1. Work with a partner.

Look at the pictures. Circle the words you see.

(ON) OFF	ON OFF	(ON OFF)
START STOP	(START STOP)	START STOP

2. Write.

Write the machines you can use.

coffee maker	copier	dishwasher	dryer
microwave oven	vacuum cleaner	washing machine	

I can use a _____

_____ .

3. Work with a partner.

Look at 2. Tell your partner the machines you can use.

36

Unit 3

Culture Note

Some technologies that are common in workplaces in this country are not common in workplaces in other countries. You may want to talk about the differences and similarities in the use of machines at work in this country and the learners' home countries.

PREPARATION

Review the new language using the following suggestions.

● Hold up word cards for **coffee maker, copier, dishwasher, dryer, microwave oven, vacuum cleaner,** and **washing machine.** Ask volunteers to read the words and then to point to the corresponding picture cards.

PRESENTATION

1. Help learners read the directions. Focus attention on the illustrations. Ask learners to say as much as they can about them. Help learners identify them. Restate learners' ideas in acceptable English and write them on the board or overhead projector. Demonstrate the activity on the board or overhead projector by circling the recognition words that appear on the TV remote control. Have learners complete the exercise in pairs. Check learners' work. Have volunteers read the answers aloud.

 2. Display pictures of machines. Talk about several machines that you can use. Demonstrate on the board or overhead projector by completing the sentence about the machines. Help learners identify machines that they can use and have them complete the sentence.

3. Help learners read the directions. Then arrange learners in pairs to read their sentences to each other. Have individuals read their sentences to the class.

FOLLOW-UP

Class Chart: Have learners work together to compile information about the whole class on a chart. Draw a 7-column chart. Write **Name** as the first column heading. Write the names of various machines in this unit as the headings for the other six columns. Have learners write their names in the first column and check off the machines that they use. Have learners examine the completed chart. Help learners draw conclusions about the types of machines that most learners use and those that learners don't use.

◆ Help the group say a few sentences summarizing the information on the class chart. Write the sentences on the board or overhead projector. Have learners copy the sentences.

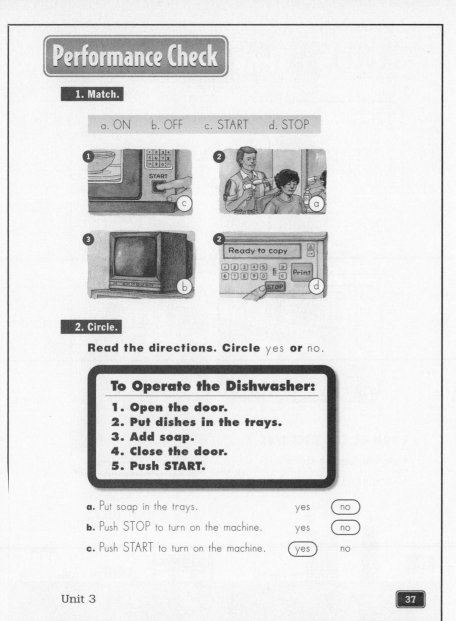

Performance Check

1. Match.

a. ON   b. OFF   c. START   d. STOP

1 — c
2 — a
3 — b
2 — d

2. Circle.

Read the directions. Circle yes **or** no.

To Operate the Dishwasher:

1. **Open the door.**
2. **Put dishes in the trays.**
3. **Add soap.**
4. **Close the door.**
5. **Push START.**

a. Put soap in the trays.   yes   (no)

b. Push STOP to turn on the machine.   yes   (no)

c. Push START to turn on the machine.   (yes)   no

Unit 3   37

ASAP
PROJECT

Help learners compile a class guidebook about operating common machines. Have each learner submit one page about a machine that he or she uses. Learners can draw or cut out magazine pictures of the machines. They can label buttons or switches that are used to turn on and off the machines and/or give other operational directions that are important. Make a copy of the guidebook for each learner.

PREPARATION

Briefly review the new language before learners open their books. Follow these suggestions.

● Write the unit recognition words **on, off, start, stop, open, close, push,** and **put in** on the board or overhead projector and perform actions related to the words, such as turning light switches on and off, starting and stopping an audio-cassette player, opening and closing a door, pushing a button or a drawer shut, and putting paper or books in a bag or briefcase. Have volunteers say the appropriate recognition words.

● Give instructions that use the words and have volunteers point to the words that are used. For example: *Please turn on the machine.* (Learners point to **on.**)

Provide specific help as needed until you are sure learners feel confident that they know all the new words.

PRESENTATION

Use any of the procedures in "Evaluation," page ix, with this page. Record individuals' results on the Unit 3 Individual Competency Chart. Record the class's results on the Class Cumulative Competency Chart.

INFORMAL WORKPLACE-SPECIFIC ASSESSMENT

Have learners name one or two machines from the unit that they see at their jobs or that are related to their career interests.

Unit 4 Overview

—SCANS Competencies—

★ Allocate time

★ Organize and maintain information

Unit 4 Workforce Skills

- Say the time, date, and day of the week
- Ask for and give personal information
- Complete a simple form

Materials

- Letter cards for **d, w, j, v,** and **y**
- Number cards for **0** through **60,** and **70, 80,** and **90**
- Word cards for **time, date, today, tomorrow, date of birth, month, year,** and for the days of the week and the months of the year
- Realia: a large wall calendar for the year, blank calendar-month grids, clocks, watches, and catalogs and advertisements from office supply stores
- Magazines or newspapers with a variety of dates
- Blackline Masters 2, 3, 4, 5, and 11

★　　★　　★　　★　　★

UNIT 4 Time Management

Look at the pictures.

Can you say the times?
Can you say the dates?

38

Unit 4

WORKFORCE SKILLS (page 38)

Say the time, date, and day of the week

★　　★　　★　　★　　★

Teaching Note

Use Blackline Masters 6 and 7: Common Directions to clarify the directions in this unit. Use page 38 to warm up learners, to draw on prior knowledge, and to spark interest.

PREPARATION

Begin the class by showing a calendar and clocks and watches. Ask learners to identify the items. Model any language they do not know.

PRESENTATION

Focus attention on the illustrations. Have learners say as much as they can about them. Learners may be able to name a few items in the pictures, but you may have to prompt them by naming items and having learners repeat. You also might read the unit title and questions aloud and have learners answer the questions. Model any words learners do not know.

You might mention places at work, such as the break room and supply room, and ask learners to raise their hands if they have seen calendars or clocks in those locations.

FOLLOW-UP

Clocks and Calendars: Provide learners with catalogs and advertisements from office supply stores. Have them find and cut out pictures of clocks and calendars. Ask if anyone can find a picture of a clock that also is a calendar (or if anyone has a watch with a calendar).

♦ Have learners share their pictures. Ask if any volunteers can say the times or dates in the pictures.

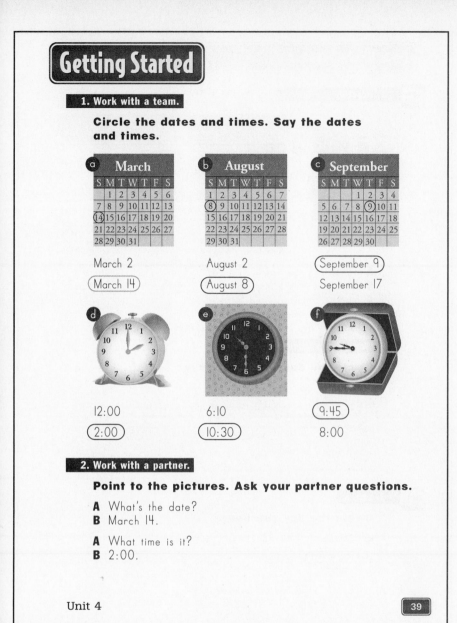

Getting Started

1. Work with a team.

Circle the dates and times. Say the dates and times.

a March

S	M	T	W	T	F	S
	1	2	3	4	5	6
7	8	9	10	11	12	13
(14)	15	16	17	18	19	20
21	22	23	24	25	26	27
28	29	30	31			

March 2
(March 14)

b August

S	M	T	W	T	F	S
1	2	3	4	5	6	7
(8)	9	10	11	12	13	14
15	16	17	18	19	20	21
22	23	24	25	26	27	28
29	30	31				

August 2
(August 8)

c September

S	M	T	W	T	F	S
		1	2	3	4
5	6	7	8	(9)	10	11
12	13	14	15	16	17	18
19	20	21	22	23	24	25
26	27	28	29	30		

(September 9)
September 17

d 12:00
(2:00)

e 6:10
(10:30)

f (9:45)
8:00

2. Work with a partner.

Point to the pictures. Ask your partner questions.

A What's the date?
B March 14.

A What time is it?
B 2:00.

Unit 4

39

Teaching Note

Use this page to introduce the new language in the unit. Whenever possible, encourage peer teaching. Supply any language learners need.

PREPARATION

Display a real calendar and clocks. Have learners identify numbers on the clocks and calandar as you point to them. Allow learners to identify other information that they may know about the clocks and calendars, such as the days of the week.

Preteach the new words in the lesson. Follow these suggestions.

● To teach the word **date,** show the current date on the calendar and say, *Today's date is (date).* Hold up the word card for **date.** Say the word and have learners repeat. Show March on the calendar and point to the date, March 2. Ask, *What's the date?* Say, *March 2.* Have learners repeat. Follow the same procedure to preteach the other answer choice dates on the page.

● To teach **time,** show the word card and have learners repeat. Focus attention on the wall clock or set the teaching clock to the current time. Ask, *What time is it?* Say, *(11:00).* Have learners repeat. Follow the same procedure to teach the times on the page.

● Preteach or review numerals **0** to **60.** For additional reinforcement, use Blackline Masters 4 and 5.

PRESENTATION

1. Help learners read the directions. Demonstrate by completing the first item on the board or overhead projector. Have learners complete the exercise in teams. Encourage learners to work together. Check the answers with the class.

2. Help learners read the directions. Model the dialogs as learners listen. Say the dialogs again and have learners repeat. Ask learners to practice the dialogs with a partner. Then model substituting the next item on the page in each dialog, and ask learners to continue similarly with the remaining items.

FOLLOW-UP

Dates and Times: Provide learners with magazines or newspapers and have them look for examples of dates and times. Learners can circle their findings. Ask volunteers to show their dates and times to the class.

◆ Display dates and times on the board or overhead projector. Say a date and have a volunteer point to the appropriate date. Repeat with the other dates and times.

Say the day of the week

★   ★   ★   ★   ★

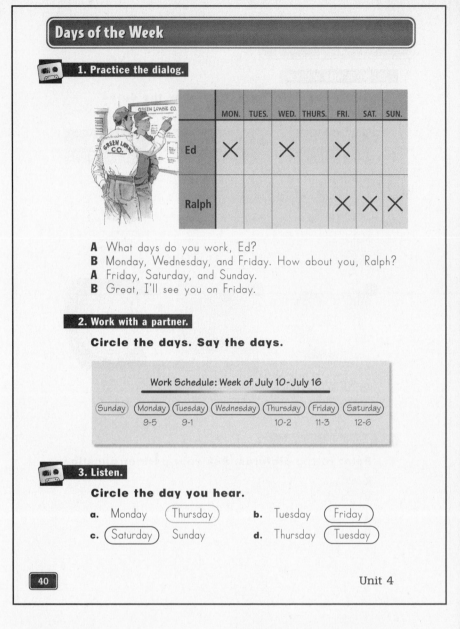

Days of the Week

 1. Practice the dialog.

	MON.	TUES.	WED.	THURS.	FRI.	SAT.	SUN.
Ed	X		X		X		
Ralph					X	X	X

A What days do you work, Ed?
B Monday, Wednesday, and Friday. How about you, Ralph?
A Friday, Saturday, and Sunday.
B Great, I'll see you on Friday.

2. Work with a partner.

Circle the days. Say the days.

Work Schedule: Week of July 10 - July 16

(Sunday) (Monday) (Tuesday) (Wednesday) (Thursday) (Friday) (Saturday)
         9-5   9-1   10-2   11-3   12-6

 3. Listen.

Circle the day you hear.

a. Monday (Thursday)   b. Tuesday (Friday)

c. (Saturday) Sunday   d. Thursday (Tuesday)

40   Unit 4

Culture Note

You might point out that English speakers usually consider Sunday the first day of the week.

PREPARATION

Preteach the new language in the lesson. Follow these suggestions.

● Focus attention on the wall calendar. Indicate each day of the week in order. Model the day and have learners repeat. Continue until learners can say the days of the week in order easily. Then hold up the word cards for the days of the week in and out of order. Ask, *What day is it?* Continue until learners can read and say the days of the week easily. See "Presenting Recognition Words" on page viii.

● Provide pairs of learners with flash cards for the days of the week. Have partners take turns holding up the cards and asking and answering, *What day is it?*

● Preteach the dialog. To teach the phrase **How about you?** choose one learner and ask, *What days do you work?* Help the learner answer. Then indicate another learner and ask, *How about you, (learner's name)?* Help the learner answer.

PRESENTATION

1. Focus attention on the illustration. Help learners identify places and objects. Have them say as much as they can about the illustration. You may want to cue them by indicating the items for learners to say, such as the bulletin board or schedule, or by saying names of items and having learners indicate them. Restate learners' ideas in acceptable English and write them on the board or overhead projector.

Present the dialog. See "Presenting Dialogs" on page viii.

2. Help learners read the directions. Demonstrate by completing the first item on the board or overhead projector and then reading the word aloud. Have learners complete the exercise in pairs. Check the exercise on the board or overhead projector.

3. Help learners read the directions. Then present the listening activity. See "Presenting Listening Activities" on page ix. Check learners' work. Ask volunteers to read their answers aloud.

4. Present or review the letters **d** and **w**. See "Presenting Letters" on page ix. Then have learners complete the exercise. Check learners' work. For

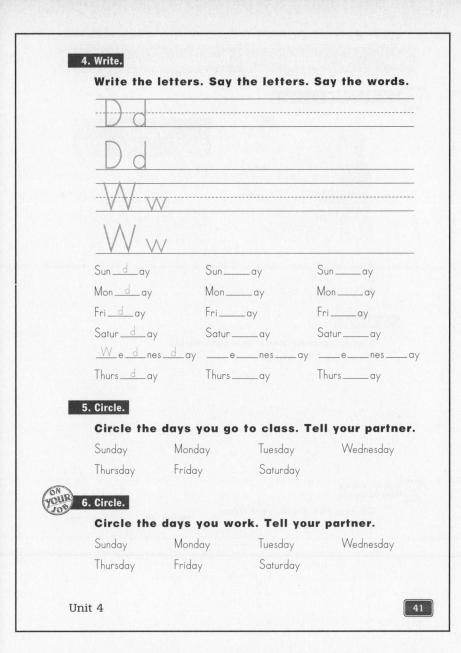

4. Write.

Write the letters. Say the letters. Say the words.

Dd

Dd

Ww

Ww

Sun_d_ay	Sun___ay	Sun___ay
Mon_d_ay	Mon___ay	Mon___ay
Fri_d_ay	Fri___ay	Fri___ay
Satur_d_ay	Satur___ay	Satur___ay
_W_e_d_nes_d_ay	___e___nes___ay	___e___nes___ay
Thurs_d_ay	Thurs___ay	Thurs___ay

5. Circle.

Circle the days you go to class. Tell your partner.

Sunday   Monday   Tuesday   Wednesday

Thursday   Friday   Saturday

 6. Circle.

Circle the days you work. Tell your partner.

Sunday   Monday   Tuesday   Wednesday

Thursday   Friday   Saturday

Unit 4   41

---

extra reinforcement, use Blackline Masters 2 and 3: Alphabet, and Blackline Master 5: Lined Paper.

Environmental Print: Have learners point out examples of words with the letters **D, d, W,** and **w** they see in the room. For more information, see "Environmental Print" on page ix.

5. Help learners read the directions. Demonstrate by completing the first item about yourself on the board or overhead projector. Then have learners complete the exercise in pairs. Check learners' work. Ask volunteers to read the answers aloud.

6. Help learners read the directions. Demonstrate by completing the first item about yourself on the board or overhead projector. Then have learners complete

the exercise in pairs. Check learners' work. Then ask volunteers to read the answers aloud.

FOLLOW-UP

Ordering the Days of the Week: Have seven learners come forward. Give each learner a different word card with a day of the week. Have learners arrange themselves in order by the day of the week. Have the rest of the class verify that the learners are in the correct order.

♦ Give each pair of learners a set of flash cards with the days of the week written on them (make flash cards on 3" by 5" cards). Have learners shuffle the cards and reorder them correctly beginning with Sunday. Have learners change partners and repeat the activity several times.

WORKFORCE SKILLS (pages 42-43)

Say the date

★   ★   ★   ★   ★

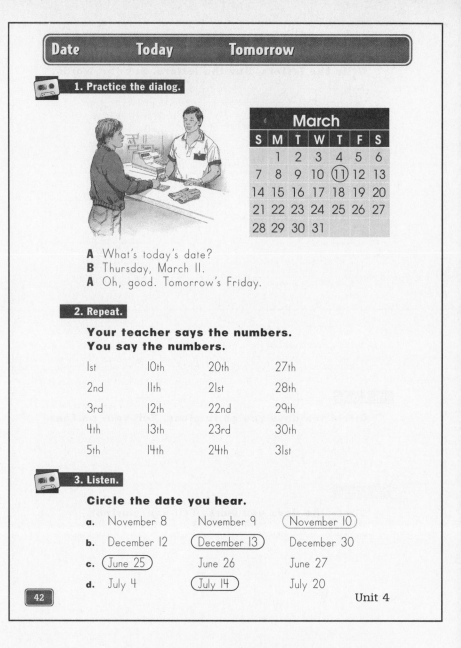

Date   Today   Tomorrow

1. Practice the dialog.

March						
S	M	T	W	T	F	S
	1	2	3	4	5	6
7	8	9	10	(11)	12	13
14	15	16	17	18	19	20
21	22	23	24	25	26	27
28	29	30	31			

A   What's today's date?
B   Thursday, March 11.
A   Oh, good. Tomorrow's Friday.

2. Repeat.

Your teacher says the numbers.
You say the numbers.

1st	10th	20th	27th
2nd	11th	21st	28th
3rd	12th	22nd	29th
4th	13th	23rd	30th
5th	14th	24th	31st

3. Listen.

Circle the date you hear.

a.   November 8   November 9   (November 10)

b.   December 12   (December 13)   December 30

c.   (June 25)   June 26   June 27

d.   July 4   (July 14)   July 20

42   Unit 4

Teaching Note

You may wish to teach the ordinal numbers and months over the course of several days rather than all at once. Begin with the current date.

PREPARATION

Preteach the new language in the lesson. Follow these suggestions.

● Teach the word **today** by saying *Today is (Thursday).* Hold up the word card for **today.** Model the word and have learners repeat. Similarly, teach the word **tomorrow.** Then teach or review **date.** Indicate the appropriate day on the calendar and say, *Today's date is (date).* Indicate the next day and say, *Tomorrow's date is (date).* Hold up the word card for **date.** Say the word and have learners repeat. See "Presenting Recognition Words" on page viii.

● Preteach the ordinal numbers. Ask, *What's today's date?* Model the answer, *Today is (date),* and have learners

repeat. Point to each day of the current month on the calendar. Model each date and have learners repeat.

● To teach the names of the months, focus attention on the calendar. Indicate and say each month in order. Have learners repeat. Then hold up word cards for the months, in and out of order, and have learners say the months. Continue until learners can read the months easily.

PRESENTATION

 1. Focus attention on the illustrations. Encourage learners to say as much as they can about the illustrations. You may want to cue them by indicating the items for them to name, or by saying names of items and having learners indicate them.

Restate their ideas in acceptable English and write them on the board or overhead projector.

Present the dialog. See "Presenting Dialogs" on page viii.

2. Write the numbers 1-31 on the board or overhead projector. Model the ordinal numbers and have learners repeat. Then point to numbers and have learners say the ordinal numbers. Next, focus learners' attention on their books. Help learners read the directions. Say each number and have learners repeat it.

 3. Help learners read the directions. Then present the listening activity. See "Presenting Listening Activities" on page ix. Check learners' work. Ask volunteers to read their answers aloud.

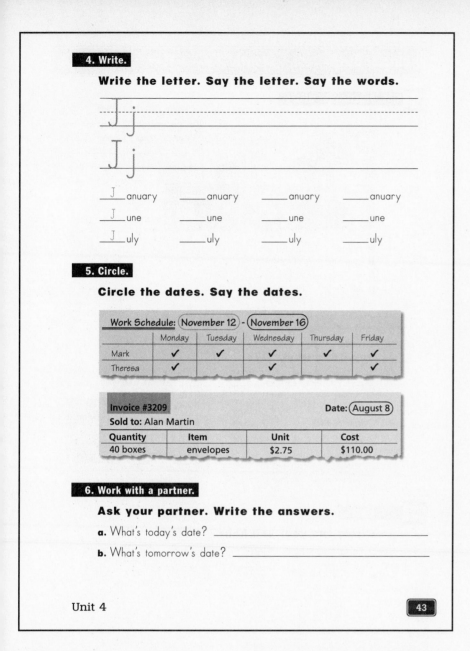

4. Write.

Write the letter. Say the letter. Say the words.

J j

J j

___anuary ___anuary ___anuary ___anuary

___une ___une ___une ___une

___uly ___uly ___uly ___uly

5. Circle.

Circle the dates. Say the dates.

Work Schedule: (November 12) - (November 16)

	Monday	Tuesday	Wednesday	Thursday	Friday
Mark	✓	✓	✓	✓	✓
Theresa	✓		✓		✓

Invoice #3209   Date: (August 8)
Sold to: Alan Martin

Quantity	Item	Unit	Cost
40 boxes	envelopes	$2.75	$110.00

6. Work with a partner.

Ask your partner. Write the answers.

a. What's today's date? _____

b. What's tomorrow's date? _____

Unit 4   43

4. Present or review the letter **j**. See "Presenting Letters" on page ix. Then have learners complete the exercise. Check learners' work. For extra reinforcement, use Blackline Master 2: Alphabet A-M and Blackline Master 5: Lined Paper.

Environmental Print: Have learners point out examples of words with **J** and **j** they see in the room. For more information, see "Environmental Print" on page ix.

5. Help learners read the directions. Demonstrate by circling the first item on the board or overhead projector. Then ask learners to complete the exercise independently. Check learners' work. Then ask volunteers to read the answers aloud.

6. Help learners read the directions. Demonstrate asking and answering the first question with a volunteer. Write the answer on the board or overhead projector. Then have learners complete the exercise. Check learners' work. Ask pairs of learners to say their questions and answers for the class.

FOLLOW-UP

Work and School Calendar: Provide learners with a blank calendar-month grid. Help learners fill in the days of the week, the numbers for the days, and the name of the current month. Tell learners to mark the days they have class with the word **class** and the days they have work with the word **work.** Ask volunteers to read some of the dates aloud that they go to class or work.

♦ Arrange learners in pairs and have them practice reading aloud the dates that they marked with **class** or **work.** Learners can compare their calendars to see if they are the same or different. Encourage learners to comment on the differences that they notice.

WORKFORCE SKILLS (pages 44-45)

Ask for and give personal information

Complete a simple form

★　　★　　★　　★　　★

Date of Birth	Month	Year

1. Practice the dialog.

January	February	March	April
May	June	July	August
September	October	November	December

A　What's your date of birth?
B　January 7, 1984.
A　Excuse me? What year?
B　1984.

2. Work with a partner.

Circle month **and** year. **Circle the dates.**
Say the dates.

Driver's License
Name: Luis Santos
Date of Birth:
July 10, 1957
month/day/year

Driver's License
Name: Elena Peters
Date of Birth:
April 5, 1943
month/day/year

 3. Listen.

Circle the year you hear.

a.　1977　1987　(1997)　　b.　1979　(1989)　2009
c.　1994　1999　(2001)　　d.　(1982)　1989　1992

44

Unit 4

PREPARATION

Preteach the new language in the lesson. Follow these suggestions.

● To teach **month** and **year,** write a few dates on the board or overhead projector. Say, *This is the month,* as you indicate the month in each date. Repeat for the year. Write additional dates on the board. Ask volunteers to come forward, one at a time, and indicate the month and year in each date.

● To teach **date of birth,** say, *My birthday is (month and day).* Write your birth month and day on the board or overhead projector and read it aloud. Then say, *My date of birth is (month, day, and year).* Write the date on the board or overhead projector and read it aloud.

● Preteach or review numerals **0** to **99.** For additional reinforcement, use Blackline Master 4: Numbers and Blackline Master 5: Lined Paper.

● Preteach the dialog. Explain that years up to 1999 are usually pronounced in two parts, with the first two numbers read together as one number and the second two read together as another number. Write **1985** on the board and model the pronunciation. Have learners repeat. To model years starting with 2000, write the years 2000, 2001, etc., on the board and model their pronunciation. Continue writing years and having learners say them until they can read the years easily. Ask volunteers to read the years aloud. Then cup your hand around your ear and ask, *Excuse me? What year?* and have learners repeat. Then say the year again.

PRESENTATION

1. Focus attention on the illustration. Have learners say as much as they can about the illustration. You may wish to cue them by indicating items for learners to name, or by saying names of items and having learners indicate them. Restate their ideas in acceptable English and write them on the board or overhead projector.

Present the dialog. See "Presenting Dialogs" on page viii.

2. Help learners read the directions. Demonstrate by circling **month** on the board or overhead projector. Then have learners complete the exercise. Check learners' work. Have volunteers say the words and dates aloud to the class.

4. Write.

Write the letters. Say the letters. Say the words.

V v

V v

Y y

Y y

No __v__ ember   No ____ ember   __y__ ear   ____ ear

Jul __y__   Jul ____   Ma __y__   Ma ____

5. Read. Write today's date.

January 7, 1984
Date of Birth

Melissa Hicks
Signature   Date

 6. Write.

Complete the form. Write about yourself.

Date of Birth

Signature   Date

Unit 4   45

Language Note

Tell learners that a date of birth includes the month, day, and year. Birthdays include only months and days.

---

 3. Help learners read the directions. Then present the listening activity. See "Presenting Listening Activities" on page ix. Check learners' work. Ask volunteers to read their answers aloud.

4. Present or review the letters **v** and **y.** See "Presenting Letters" on page ix. Then have learners complete the exercise. Check learners' work. For extra reinforcement, use Blackline Master 3: Alphabet N-Z and Blackline Master 5: Lined Paper.

Environmental Print: Have learners point out examples of words with the letters **V, v, Y,** and **y** they see in the room. For more information, see "Environmental Print" on page ix.

5. Help learners read the directions. Ask learners today's date. Demonstrate by filling in the current date on the board or overhead projector. Then have learners complete the exercise independently. Check learners' work.

 6. Help learners read the directions. Demonstrate by completing the form about yourself on the board or overhead projector. To teach **signature,** print your name on the board. Then write **Signature** on the board, and sign your name after it. Have students compare the printed name and your signature. Then have learners practice writing their signatures on sheets of paper. Next, have learners complete the activity. Check learners' work. Ask volunteers to read their answers aloud.

FOLLOW-UP

Closed December 25: Ask learners what days they don't work or go to class. You may want to display the large wall calendar and point out days as learners mention them. If learners don't mention holidays, point them out and explain that many workplaces are closed on holidays. Together, make a list of dates for the holidays. Encourage learners to tell if they work or not on those days.

♦ Have learners talk about holidays that are celebrated in their native countries. Help learners point to the holidays on the wall calendar.

★　　★　　★　　★　　★

Time

 1. Practice the dialog.

A What time is it?
B It's 1:30.
A Excuse me? 1:30?
B Yes, that's right.

2. Work with a partner.

Say the times.

a. It's 9:00.　　**b.** It's 3:15.　　**c.** It's 2:30.

d. It's 7:45.　　**e.** It's 5:10.　　**f.** It's 11:40.

46

Unit 4

Teaching Note

You may want to use several lessons to teach learners to tell time.

PREPARATION

Preteach the new language in the lesson. Follow these suggestions.

● Use the word card, realia clocks and watches, and the illustrations on the page to preteach or review the recognition word **time.** Follow the procedure on page 39. See "Presenting Recognition Words" on page viii.

● Use an analog clock with movable hands or Blackline Master 11: Clock to teach or review telling time. First, set the clock to an hour. Say, *It's (nine) o'clock* and have learners repeat. Proceed through the hours in order, then out of order, until learners name the hour easily. Repeat the procedure for some half-hour, quarter-hour, and five-minute intervals, saying *It's (nine-o-five, nine-fifteen, nine-thirty).*

● Preteach the dialog. Set the hands of the analog clock to 1:30. Point to the clock and ask, *What time is it?* Have learners repeat. Model the answer, *It's 1:30.* Follow the procedure on page 44 to review the question *Excuse me?* Then ask, *Excuse me? 1:30?* and have learners repeat. Then say, *Yes, that's right.* Have learners repeat.

PRESENTATION

 1. Focus attention on the illustration. Have learners say as much as they can about it. You may want to cue them by indicating the items for learners to say, or by saying names of items and having learners indicate them. Restate their ideas in acceptable English and write them on the board or overhead projector.

Present the dialog. See "Presenting Dialogs" on page viii.

2. Help learners read the directions. Demonstrate by saying the time of the first item. Have learners repeat. Then have learners complete the exercise in pairs. Have volunteers say the times aloud to the class.

3. Help learners read the directions. Then present the listening activity. See "Presenting Listening Activities" on page ix. Check learners' work. Ask volunteers to read their answers aloud.

4. Help learners read the directions. Demonstrate by circling the first time on the board or overhead projector. Then have learners complete the exercise independently. Check learners' work. Ask volunteers to say the times aloud.

3. Listen.

Circle the time you hear.

a. (4:00) 5:00 8:00   b. 5:30 6:30 (7:30)

c. 11:15 (12:15) 4:15   d. (5:45) 7:45 9:45

4. Circle.

Circle the times. Say the times.

Time Card

Name:	Wanda Chin	Employee #: 3228
Date	Time In	Time Out
April 2	(7:22)	(3:35)
April 3	(7:31)	(3:30)

5. Write.

Write the times.
Ask and say the times with your partner.

a. __4:15__   b. __9:30__   c. __2:45__

6. Ask your partner the time.

Unit 4   47

Language Note

Tell learners that A.M. indicates times from midnight until 12 noon and P.M. indicates times from 12 noon until midnight.

5. Help learners read the directions. Demonstrate by completing the first item on the board or overhead projector. Then ask learners to complete the exercise independently. Write the answers on the board or overhead projector. Have learners ask and say the times with a partner. Then ask volunteers to say the times aloud.

6. Help learners read the directions. Model by asking a learner to say the time. Then have learners work with partners to complete the activity. Have learners switch partners several times and repeat the activity. Invite pairs to repeat their conversations to the class.

FOLLOW-UP

More Clocks: Arrange learners in pairs. Give each learner a copy of Blackline Master 11: Clock. Have learners take turns setting times on their clocks and asking their partners the time. Have learners change partners and repeat the activity.

♦ Have learners take turns setting different times on their clocks for their partners to say and write.

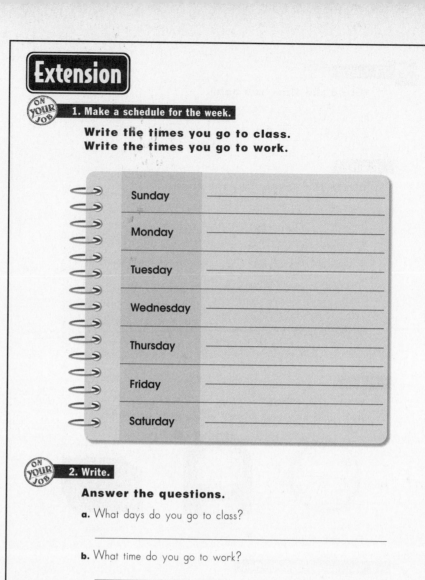

Extension

1. Make a schedule for the week.

Write the times you go to class.
Write the times you go to work.

Sunday _____

Monday _____

Tuesday _____

Wednesday _____

Thursday _____

Friday _____

Saturday _____

2. Write.

Answer the questions.

a. What days do you go to class?

_____

b. What time do you go to work?

_____

48

Unit 4

SCANS Note

You may want to point out to learners that different workplaces often use different types of work schedules. For example, some workplaces use schedules that change every week, every two weeks, or every month. To work in one of these environments, it's important for workers to be flexible about when they can work. Ask learners if they have a flexible work schedule.

PREPARATION

Refer to the wall calendar. Ask, *What day is it today? What day is it tomorrow? What days do we have class? What days do you go to work?* Encourage a variety of responses.

PRESENTATION

 1. Help learners read the directions. Demonstrate on the board or overhead projector, using personal or fictitious information as an example. Have learners complete the activity. Check learners' work.

 2. Help learners read the directions. Demonstrate by completing the items on the board or overhead projector. Then have learners complete the items independently. Check

learners' work. Have volunteers read their answers aloud.

FOLLOW-UP

Interviews: Arrange learners in pairs to interview each other about their schedules. Have them ask each other, for each day of the week, *What do you do on (Monday)?* Have learners change partners and repeat the activity. Have volunteers say their conversations for the class.

♦ Have each learner tell the class what his or her partner does on a certain day.

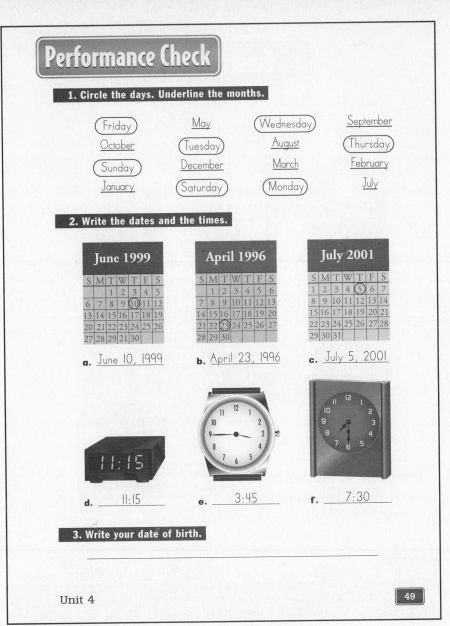

Performance Check

1. Circle the days. Underline the months.

Friday   May   Wednesday   September

October   Tuesday   August   Thursday

Sunday   December   March   February

January   Saturday   Monday   July

2. Write the dates and the times.

June 1999

S	M	T	W	T	F	S
		1	2	3	4	5
6	7	8	9	10	11	12
13	14	15	16	17	18	19
20	21	22	23	24	25	26
27	28	29	30			

a. June 10, 1999

April 1996

S	M	T	W	T	F	S
	1	2	3	4	5	6
7	8	9	10	11	12	13
14	15	16	17	18	19	20
21	22	23	24	25	26	27
28	29	30				

b. April 23, 1996

July 2001

S	M	T	W	T	F	S
1	2	3	4	5	6	7
8	9	10	11	12	13	14
15	16	17	18	19	20	21
22	23	24	25	26	27	28
29	30	31				

c. July 5, 2001

d. 11:15

e. 3:45

f. 7:30

3. Write your date of birth.

Unit 4   49

ASAP PROJECT

A Class Calendar: With the class, brainstorm dates and events during the present month that are important for members of the class, such as training sessions, work, vacations, holidays, birthdays, and appointments. Have learners fill in the events on a large wall calendar. Learners should copy dates relevant to them onto a blank calendar-month grid supplied by the teacher. Learners can include the times for the activities on their calendars.

Refer to the learners' calendars throughout the month and discuss the events and activities.

PREPARATION

Use a calendar to review the days of the week and the months of the year. Point out several dates on the calendar. Ask volunteers to write them on the board or overhead projector.

Have learners write their dates of birth on sheets of paper. Ask volunteers to read their dates aloud to the class.

Use an analog clock or Blackline Master 11: Clock. Set the clock to different times. Have learners say the times aloud and write them on the board or overhead projector.

Provide specific help as needed until you are sure learners feel confident that they know all the new words.

PRESENTATION

Use any of the procedures in "Evaluation," page ix, with this page. Record individuals' results on the Unit 4 Individual Competency Chart. Record the class's results on the Class Cumulative Competency Chart.

INFORMAL WORKPLACE-SPECIFIC ASSESSMENT

Ask learners to say the days they work and have class this week. Ask them what time they go to work.

Unit 5 Overview

—SCANS Competencies—

★ Serve clients/customers

★ Monitor and correct performance

★ Understand organizational systems

★ Interpret and communicate
information

Unit 5 Workforce Skills

● Recognize good customer service

● Greet customers

● Take customer orders

● Offer assistance to customers

● Apologize and correct errors

Materials

● Letter cards for **h, i, g, x,** and **f**

● Magazines/catalogs with pictures
of workers assisting customers

● Word cards for **customer service,
exchange, refund, please, thank
you, hello, sorry, goodbye,** and
receipt

● Realia or picture cards for a coffee
cup; a car battery; machines and
appliances such as a telephone, a
copier, and a coffee maker; a notebook with a price tag for $10; supplies
(gloves, towels, paper, envelopes, and
bags) with price tags; receipts; return
forms; and stamps

● Blackline Masters 2, 3, 5, and 12

★   ★   ★   ★   ★

U N I T **5**   **Customer Service**

Look at the pictures.

Who are the workers?

Who are the customers?

Are the workers doing a
good job?

50

Unit 5

WORKFORCE SKILLS (page 50)

Recognize good customer service

★   ★   ★   ★   ★

Teaching Note

*Use Blackline Masters 6 and 7: Common
Directions to clarify the directions in this
unit. Use page 50 to warm up learners,
to check and draw on prior knowledge,
and to spark interest.*

PRESENTATION

Focus attention on the illustrations. Have
learners say as much as they can about
them. Learners may be able to name a
few items in the pictures, but you may
have to prompt them by naming items,
locations, and occupations and having
learners repeat. Help learners identify

who are the workers and who are the
customers. Ask learners to speculate about
what the customers want. You also might
read the unit title and questions aloud and
have learners answer the questions. Model
any words learners do not know.

You might mention how the workers
help customers in the workplaces.

FOLLOW-UP

Magazine Pictures: Provide pairs
of learners with magazines that have
pictures of people at work. Ask learners to cut out pictures of workers
and customers. Have each pair of
learners show their pictures to the
class and identify the workers and
the customers. Encourage them to say
if the workers are doing a good job.

♦ Have pairs of learners join together to
make groups of four. Ask each pair to
show their pictures to the other pair and
identify the workers and the customers.

Getting Started

1. Work with a team.

Are the workers doing a good job? Circle yes **or** no.

a. (yes) no   **b.** yes (no)

c. (yes) no   **d.** yes (no)

2. Work with a partner.

Point to the pictures. Ask your partner questions.

A Is he doing a good job?
B Yes.

Unit 5

51

Teaching Note

Use this page to introduce the new language in the unit. Whenever possible, encourage peer teaching. Supply any language the learners need.

PREPARATION

Focus attention on the illustrations. Have learners say as much as they can about them. Learners may be able to name a few items in the pictures, but you may have to prompt them by naming items, locations, and occupations and having learners repeat. Help learners identify who are the workers and who are the customers. Ask learners to speculate about what the customers want. Have learners identify or comment on other workers and customers that they know about at their own worksites.

If necessary, preteach **doing a good job** by pantomiming ignoring a customer. Say, *Am I doing a good job?* Write the question on the board and have learners repeat. Then say, *No.* Next pantomime paying attention to a customer and say,

Am I doing a good job? pointing to the words on the board. Ask a volunteer to answer.

PRESENTATION

1. Help learners read the directions. Demonstrate by completing the first item on the board or overhead projector. Then have learners complete the exercise in teams. Encourage learners to work together. Go over the answers with the class.

2. Help learners read the directions. Model the dialog as learners listen. Say the dialog again and have learners repeat. Ask learners to practice the dialog with a partner. Then model substituting the next item on the page in the dialog, and ask learners to continue similarly with the remaining items.

FOLLOW-UP

Have learners suggest words to describe behaviors that show good customer service. Some words might be: **listen, help, smile,** and **nice.** Create a list on the board.

♦ Have learners choose a word and illustrate it or find a magazine picture that represents the meaning of the word. Display the list and pictures for reference throughout the unit.

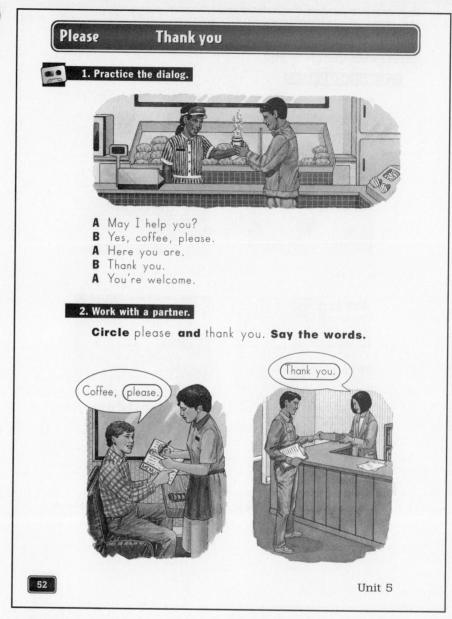

Please   Thank you

1. Practice the dialog.

A   May I help you?
B   Yes, coffee, please.
A   Here you are.
B   Thank you.
A   You're welcome.

2. Work with a partner.

Circle please **and** thank you. **Say the words.**

Coffee, please.

Thank you.

52   Unit 5

Language Note

*In addition to the phrases on this page, you may want to model and have learners practice other phrases commonly used to offer assistance, such as **Can I help you?** You might also present additional greetings, such as **Good morning** and **Good afternoon.***

PREPARATION

Preteach the new language in the lesson. Follow these suggestions.

• Use word cards and pantomime to preteach the words **please** and **thank you.** See "Presenting Recognition Words" on page viii.

• Preteach the dialog. If necessary, introduce the phrases **May I help you?** and **Here you are.** Pantomime holding an order pad with a pencil poised over it. Ask, *May I help you?* Model the question and have learners repeat. Then show a real cup of coffee and model the answer, *Yes, coffee, please.* Have learners repeat. Pantomime giving the coffee and say, *Here you are.* Have learners repeat.

PRESENTATION

1. Focus attention on the illustration. Help learners identify the place, the worker, and the customer. Have them say as much as they can about the illustration. You may also want to name items in the illustration and have learners point to them. Restate learners' ideas in acceptable English and write them on the board or overhead projector.

Then present the dialog. See "Presenting Dialogs" on page viii.

2. Help learners read the directions. Demonstrate the first item by circling **please** and then reading the word aloud. Then have learners complete the exercise in pairs.

3. Help learners read the directions. Then present the listening activity. See "Presenting Listening Activities" on page ix. Check learners' work. Ask volunteers to read their answers aloud.

4. Help learners read the directions. Demonstrate by completing the first item on the board or overhead projector. Have learners complete the exercise in pairs. Check the exercise on the board or overhead projector.

5. Help learners read the directions. You may want to bring in some stamps. Then demonstrate by completing the first item on the board or overhead projector. Have learners complete the exercise independently. Ask several learners to read their answers aloud.

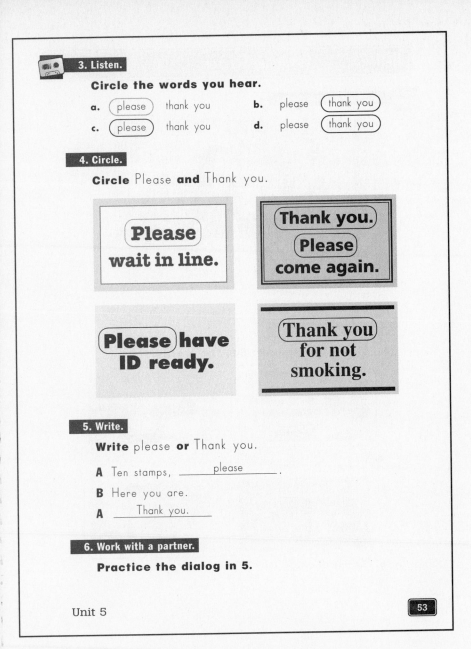

3. Listen.

Circle the words you hear.

a. (please) thank you   b. please (thank you)

c. (please) thank you   d. please (thank you)

4. Circle.

Circle Please **and** Thank you.

(Please)
wait in line.

(Thank you.)
(Please)
come again.

(Please)have
ID ready.

(Thank you)
for not
smoking.

5. Write.

Write please **or** Thank you.

A Ten stamps, _____please_____.

B Here you are.

A _____Thank you._____

6. Work with a partner.

Practice the dialog in 5.

Unit 5   **53**

---

6. Review the dialog in item 5 with the class. Then have learners practice the dialog in pairs, switching roles and changing partners several times. Have several pairs say the dialog aloud for the class.

FOLLOW-UP

Following Instructions: Display a number of common objects (such as pencils, books, cups, towels, and note-books) on a table or desk. Have a volunteer role-play a worker standing behind the table or desk. Ask others to come up and ask the worker for one or more of the items. The worker should find the object and give it to the other learner. Remind learners to use **please** and **thank you.**

♦ If possible, ask learners to go to a local post office or store to buy stamps outside of class. Beforehand, talk about the price of stamps. Have learners change the first line of the dialog to reflect the number of stamps they would like. Then have learners practice their lines until they feel comfortable. Learners may want to go in pairs to make the purchase. Later, have learners report back about the event. Did they have any problems? Was it easy or difficult to understand the clerk?

WORKFORCE SKILLS (pages 54-55)

Greet customers

Offer assistance to customers

★　　★　　★　　★　　★

SCANS Note

As you work through this unit, point out to learners that customer service providers include retail and food service workers as well as providers of medical services, legal services, auto repair work, banking services, and most other services. Encourage learners to identify the customers at their workplaces.

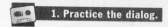

| Hello | Customer Service |

1. Practice the dialog.

A Hello, may I help you?
B Yes, this telephone doesn't work.
A OK, please take it to Customer Service.
B Thank you.

2. Work with a partner.

Circle the picture. Say the words.

a. Hello

b. Customer Service

54   Unit 5

PREPARATION

Preteach the new language in the lesson. Follow these suggestions.

• Use word cards, pictures, and gestures to preteach the words **hello** and **customer service**. See "Presenting Recognition Words" on page viii.

• Preteach the dialog. Review **May I help you?** using the procedure on page 52. Then display a broken machine or picture of a machine and say, *This (telephone) doesn't work.* Have learners repeat. Then model the answer, *OK, please take it to Customer Service.* Have learners repeat.

PRESENTATION

1. Focus attention on the illustration. Help learners identify the place and the people. Have them say as much as they can about the illustration. You may want to indicate items for learners to name, or say names of items and have learners indicate them. Restate their ideas in acceptable English and write them on the board or overhead projector.

Present the dialog. See "Presenting Dialogs" on page viii.

2. Help learners read the directions. Demonstrate by completing the first item on the board or overhead projector. Then have learners complete the exercise in pairs. Check the exercise on the board or overhead projector. Have volunteers read the words aloud.

3. Help learners read the directions. Then present the listening activity. See "Presenting Listening Activities" on page ix. Check learners' work. Ask volunteers to read their answers aloud.

4. Present or review the letters **h** and **i.** See "Presenting Letters" on page ix. Then have learners complete the exercise. Check learners' work. For extra reinforcement, use Blackline Master 2: Alphabet A-M and Blackline Master 5: Lined Paper.

Environmental Print: Have learners point out examples of words with the letters **H, h, I,** and **i** they see in the room. For more information, see "Environmental Print" on page ix.

Write the letters. Say the letters. Say the words.

X x

X x

F f

F f

E X CHANGE   E ___ CHANGE   O F F O ___ ___

e x change   e ___ change   e X it   e ___ it

co f f ee   co ___ ___ ee   re f und   re ___ und

5. Write.

Get a refund. Complete the refund form.

Customer Name:_____ Date:_____

Address:_____

City:_____ State:_____ Zip Code:_____

Telephone Number:_____

Item: **Dryer**

Date of Purchase: **May 20**

Mark (X) one: Exchange ( ) Refund (**X**)

Amount: **$250.00**

Unit 5

59

---

5. Help learners read the directions. Demonstrate by completing the form on the board or overhead projector using your own or fictitious information. Then have learners complete the activity. Check learners' work. Ask volunteers to read the answers aloud.

FOLLOW-UP

Filling Out Refund Forms: Bring in receipts from various stores and products. You might copy them or enlarge them so learners can read them easily. Have each learner select an item. Distribute copies of a simple refund form similar to the one in the book. Ask learners to work in pairs to help each other fill out refund forms for the products. Check learners' work.

♦ Arrange learners in small groups. Have them take turns sharing the receipts and refund forms and reading their forms aloud.

Write.

**The microwave oven doesn't work. Get a refund.
Complete the form. Use the receipt.**

HOME STORE

Microwave oven $75.00

Total $75.00

March 5   16:43

HOME STORE
RETURN REQUEST FORM

Date:_____

Customer Name:_____

Address:_____

City:_____ State:_____ Zip Code:_____

Telephone Number:_____

Item: _Microwave oven_____

Date of Purchase: _March 5_____

Exchange ( ) Refund (X)

Amount: _$75.00_

Unit 5

PREPARATION

Review the new language using the following suggestions.

• Review **exchange** and **refund** using the procedure on page 58.

• Hold up the word card for **receipt** and a receipt. Model the word **receipt** and have learners repeat. Help learners find important information on the receipt such as the name of the store, the date of purchase, and the price of an item. Encourage learners to share information they know about receipts.

PRESENTATION

Help learners read the directions. Focus attention on the microwave oven, the receipt, and the return form. Ask learners to say as much as they can about

them. Restate learners' ideas in acceptable English and write them on the board or overhead projector. Demonstrate by completing the first part of the return form on the board or overhead projector. Have learners complete the exercise independently. Check learners' work. Have volunteers read aloud the information they wrote on the return form.

FOLLOW-UP

Return Role Play: Set up a customer service area in the room with a counter and refund and exchange forms. Use the word card for **customer service** to identify the area. Have a volunteer role-play a customer service worker. Play the role of a customer coming to exchange a broken appliance. Invite other volunteers

to role-play other customers wanting refunds and exchanges. You may want to distribute cards to "the customers" with names of appliances or supplies and the reasons for returning them. Provide a similar set (without problems), as well as play money, to the customer service worker.

♦ Help the class look through the refund forms and determine how many exchanges were made and how many refunds were made. Help the class prepare a chart showing the number of each kind of transaction in the role play.

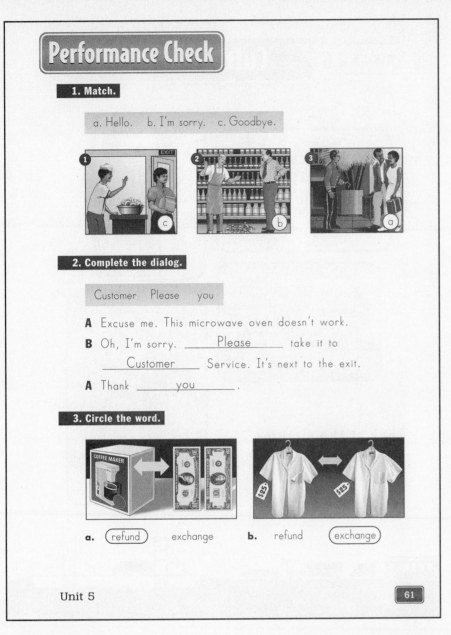

Performance Check

1. Match.

a. Hello. b. I'm sorry. c. Goodbye.

1 c
2 b
3 a

2. Complete the dialog.

Customer   Please   you

A Excuse me. This microwave oven doesn't work.

B Oh, I'm sorry. _____Please_____ take it to
_____Customer_____ Service. It's next to the exit.

A Thank _____you_____.

3. Circle the word.

COFFEE MAKER

a. (refund)   exchange   **b.** refund   (exchange)

Unit 5

61

ASAP PROJECT

As a group, brainstorm a list of useful phrases for talking to customers. Learners can look through the unit for ideas. You may want to introduce additional phrases, such as **Can I help you?** and **Come again.** Ask learners to choose one of the phrases and draw or find a magazine picture that shows a situation when the phrase might be used. Learners can add a speech bubble to the appropriate speaker and write the expression in it. Compile the pages to form a booklet. If possible, duplicate the booklet so each learner has a copy.

PREPARATION

Briefly review the new language before learners open their books. Follow these suggestions.

● Write the recognition words on the board or overhead projector. Ask volunteers to act out situations related to the words. You may want to supply them with picture cards of purchases and play money (using Blackline Master 12: Money) to act out getting a refund or making an exchange. Have volunteers say the appropriate words.

● Say sentences or expressions that use the words and have volunteers point to the correct words that they hear. For example: *Hello. May I help you? I'm sorry. I made a mistake* or *You're welcome. Goodbye.*

Provide specific help as needed until you are sure learners feel confident that they know all the new words.

PRESENTATION

Use any of the procedures in "Evaluation," page ix, with this page. Record individuals' results on the Unit 5 Individual Competency Chart. Record the class's results on the Class Cumulative Competency Chart.

INFORMAL WORKPLACE-SPECIFIC ASSESSMENT

Ask learners to role-play greeting a customer at their workplace.

Unit 6 Overview
—SCANS Competencies—

★ Understand social and organizational systems

★ Participate as a member of a team

★ Allocate time

★ Acquire and evaluate information

Unit 6 Workforce Skills

● Report lateness or absence

● Understand company rules

● Understand good work habits

● Use public transportation to get to work

Materials

● Letter cards for **q, z, k,** and **b**

● Picture cards, word cards, and/or realia for **take, the bus, walk, drive,** and **goggles**

● Word cards for **on time, early, late, understand, repeat, quiet, careful,** and **work zone**

● Pictures or realia of safety equipment (gloves, a hard hat, work boots); a supply room; a TV; a worksite with hazards such as sharp objects, electrical outlets, etc.; a picture of someone doing something dangerous

● Realia: a clock with moveable hands, telephones

● Blackline Masters 2, 3, 5, 10, and 11

★   ★   ★   ★   ★

UNIT 6   Culture of Work

Look at the pictures.
Where are the people?

What are they doing?

WORK ZONE

COUNTY GENERAL HOSPITAL

62

Unit 6

WORKFORCE SKILLS (page 62)

Understand company rules

Understand good work habits

★   ★   ★   ★   ★

Teaching Note

Use Blackline Masters 6 and 7: Common Directions to clarify the directions in this unit. Use this page to warm up learners, to draw on prior knowledge, and to spark interest.

PRESENTATION

Focus attention on the illustrations. Have learners say as much as they can about them. Learners may be able to name a few items in the pictures, but you may have to prompt them by naming items, locations, and occupations and having

learners repeat. You also might read the unit title and questions aloud and have learners answer the questions. Model any language learners need.

FOLLOW-UP

Class Poll: Write the modes of transportation pictured in a list on the board. Elicit other modes of transportation from the class and add them to the list. Help learners say the different words listed.

◆ Distribute blank copies of a two-column chart to the class. Ask learners to copy the list of transportation words in the first column. You may need to demonstrate this on the board or overhead projector. Then have learners circulate and find a classmate who has used each type of transportation. The classmate can write his or her name next to the word.

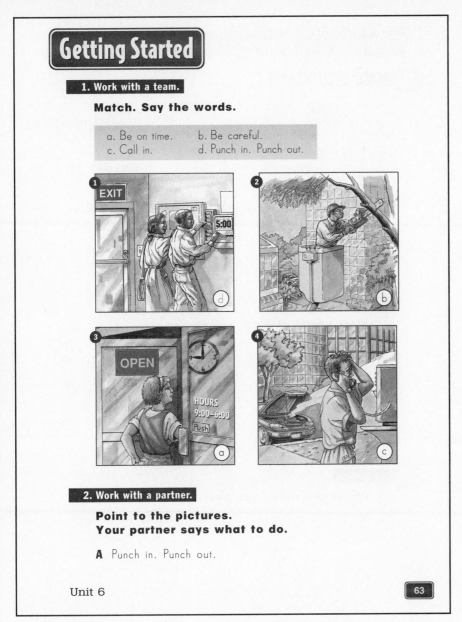

Teaching Note

Use this page to introduce the new language in the unit. Whenever possible, encourage peer teaching. Supply any language learners need.

PREPARATION

Focus attention on the illustrations. Have learners say as much as they can about them. Learners may be able to name a few items in the pictures, but you may have to prompt them by naming items, locations, and occupations and having learners repeat.

Preteach the new language in the lesson. Follow these suggestions.

● To teach **Be on time**, write 9:00 on the board or overhead projector. Say, *Work starts at 9:00. Be here by 9:00. Be here on time.* Hold up the word card for **on time** and model the expression. Have learners repeat.

PRESENTATION

1. Help learners read the directions. Demonstrate by completing the first item on the board or overhead projector. Have learners complete the exercise in teams. Encourage learners to work together. Go over the answers with the class.

2. Help learners read the directions. Model the expression as learners listen. Say the expression again and have learners repeat. Ask learners to practice the first item with a partner. Then model substituting the next item on the page in the activity, and ask learners to continue similarly with the remaining items.

FOLLOW-UP

Act It Out: Divide the class into groups. Have each group act out a situation involving one of the expressions on the page. Have the other groups figure out which expression their classmates are acting out.

◆ Have learners write the rule their classmates are acting out.

WORKFORCE SKILLS (pages 64-65)

Report lateness or absence

★　　★　　★　　★　　★

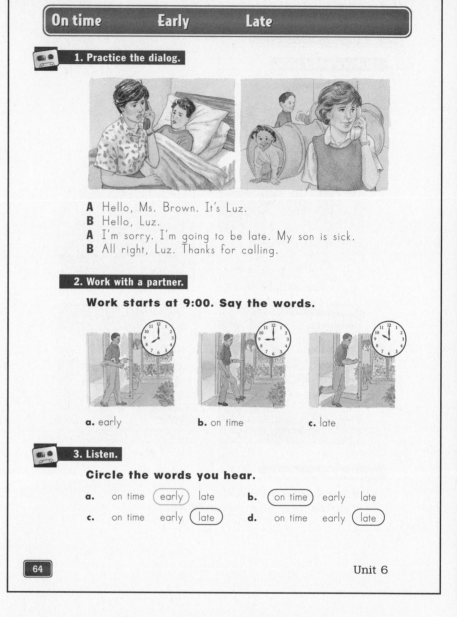

On time　　Early　　Late

1. Practice the dialog.

A Hello, Ms. Brown. It's Luz.
B Hello, Luz.
A I'm sorry. I'm going to be late. My son is sick.
B All right, Luz. Thanks for calling.

2. Work with a partner.

Work starts at 9:00. Say the words.

a. early　　　**b.** on time　　　**c.** late

3. Listen.

Circle the words you hear.

a. on time (early) late　　**b.** (on time) early late

c. on time early (late)　　**d.** on time early (late)

64　　　　　　　　　　　　　　　　　　　　　　　Unit 6

Teaching Note

You may want to bring in telephone receivers, play telephones, or copies of Blackline Master 10: Telephone for learners to use while acting out the dialog on this page.

PREPARATION

Preteach or review the new language in the lesson. Follow these suggestions.

● Use clocks, word cards, and pantomime to preteach or review the recognition words **on time, early,** and **late.** See "Presenting Recognition Words" on page viii.

● Preteach the dialog. Introduce the phrase **My son is sick.** Draw or show a picture of a sick boy. Say, *My son is sick.* Have learners repeat.

PRESENTATION

 1. Focus attention on the illustration. Help learners identify where the people are and what they are talking about. Have them say as much as they can about the illustration. You may want to cue them by indicating the items for learners to say, or by saying names of items and having learners indicate them. Restate learners' ideas in acceptable English and write them on the board or overhead projector.

Present the dialog. See "Presenting Dialogs" on page viii.

2. Help learners read the directions. Model the first item by reading the word aloud. Then have learners complete the exercise in pairs.

 3. Help learners read the directions. Then present the listening activity. See "Presenting Listening Activities" on page ix. Check learners' work. Ask volunteers to read their answers aloud.

4. Help learners read the directions. Demonstrate by completing the first item on the board or overhead projector. Then have learners complete the exercise independently. Check learners' work. Have learners read the words aloud to a partner. For extra reinforcement, use Blackline Master 5: Lined Paper.

5. Help learners read the directions. Demonstrate by completing the first item on the board or overhead projector. Then ask learners to complete the exercise independently. Check learners' work. Then ask volunteers to read the answers aloud.

4. Write.

Write the words. Say the words.

on time	_____	_____
late	_____	_____
early	_____	_____

5. Write.

Work starts at 8:30.
Write late, early, **or** on time. **Say the words.**

a. ___on time___   b. ___early___   c. ___late___

6. Write.

Write the time. Write on time, late, **or** early.

I start work at _____ . I start work _____ .

7. Write.

You're late for class or work. Who do you call?
Write the name and number.

Name: _____

Telephone number: _____

Unit 6   65

---

6. Help learners read the directions. Demonstrate completing the sentences about yourself. Then have learners complete the sentences about themselves. Check learners' answers. Invite volunteers to read the sentences aloud to the class.

7. Help learners read the directions. Demonstrate filling in the information about yourself on the board or overhead projector. Ask learners to say who they will call and what number they will dial. Have learners fill in the information. Help learners as needed.

FOLLOW-UP

Calling In: Have pairs role-play calling their bosses to report being late or absent. Have pairs present their role plays to the class.

♦ As a group, brainstorm lists of good and bad reasons for being absent or late. Then expand the role-play activity by encouraging learners to supply more information in the dialog. Learners can say when they expect to arrive at work and why they will be late/absent.

WORKFORCE SKILLS (pages 66-67)

Understand good work habits

★   ★   ★   ★   ★

SCANS Note

Emphasize the importance of asking questions and clarifying instructions. Explain that a good way to show that you understand instructions is by nodding your head or saying OK.

Understand   Repeat

1. Practice the dialog.

A Please take the TVs to the supply room.
B I'm sorry. I don't understand. Can you repeat that?
A Take the TVs to the supply room.
B Oh, OK.

2. Write.

Write the words. Say the words.

I don't __understand__ .   I don't _____ .

I don't _____ .   I don't _____ .

Can you __repeat__ that?   Can you _____ that?

Can you _____ that?   Can you _____ that?

3. Listen.

Do you hear repeat? **Circle** yes **or** no.

a. (yes) no   **b.** yes (no)

c. yes (no)   **d.** (yes) no

e. yes (no)   **f.** (yes) no

66   Unit 6

PREPARATION

Preteach the new language in the lesson. Follow these suggestions.

● Preteach or review the words **understand** and **repeat.** To preteach the word **understand**, say, *I understand English.* Write the sentence on the board and have learners repeat. Then say, *I don't understand (Greek).* Have learners say languages they don't understand. To preteach **repeat**, ask a volunteer, *What's your telephone number?* After the learner says the number, say, *Can you repeat that?* Help the learner repeat the telephone number. See "Presenting Recognition Words" on page viii.

● Preteach the dialog. Display a picture of a TV and a picture of a supply room and say, *Please take the TV to the supply room.* Look confused and say, *I don't*

understand. Can you repeat that? Have learners repeat. Model again the request, *Take the TV to the supply room* and have learners repeat. Then carry a picture of a TV to an area labeled "Supply Room" to clarify the meaning of **take.** Say, *I'm taking the TV to the supply room.*

PRESENTATION

  1. Focus attention on the illustration. Help learners speculate about the people, workplace, and items in the workplace. Have them say as much as they can about the illustration. You may want to cue them by indicating the items for learners to say, or by saying names of items and having learners indicate them. Restate their ideas in acceptable English and write them on the board or overhead projector.

Present the dialog. See "Presenting Dialogs" on page viii.

2. Help learners read the directions. Demonstrate by completing the first item on the board or overhead projector. Say the sentence. Then have learners complete the exercise independently. Check the exercise on the board or overhead projector. Have volunteers read the sentences aloud.

  3. Help learners read the directions. Then present the listening activity. See "Presenting Listening Activities" on page ix. Check learners' work. Ask volunteers to read their answers aloud.

4. Focus attention on the illustrations. Help learners identify the people, workplaces, and items in the workplaces. Have them say as much as

English ASAP

Write understand **or** repeat.

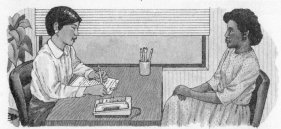

A What's your telephone number?

B 555-3498.

A I'm sorry. Can you _____repeat_____ that?

B 555-3498.

A Thank you.

A Can you help me?

B Sure, what's the matter?

A I don't _____understand_____ how to use this machine.

B I'll help you.

A Thank you.

5. Work with a partner.

Practice the dialogs in 4.

Unit 6

67

---

they can about the illustrations. Point out that in the second illustration, one worker doesn't understand the machine and the second worker is going to press the buttons on the machine for her. Then help learners read the directions. Demonstrate by completing the first dialog on the board or overhead projector. Then ask learners to complete the exercise in pairs. Check learners' work.

5. Help learners read the directions. Demonstrate the activity with a volunteer. Then have learners complete the activity in pairs. Invite pairs to present the dialogs to the class.

FOLLOW-UP

I Don't Understand: Give a series of commands for learners to follow. For example, say, *Put the red book on the shelf.* Learners can respond by following the command, or by saying, *I don't understand. Can you repeat that?* If they don't understand, repeat the instruction.

♦ Have pairs of learners take turns giving each other instructions and asking for clarification and repetition. Have learners change partners and repeat the activity. Ask several pairs to present their exchanges to the class.

WORKFORCE SKILLS (pages 68-69)

Understand company rules

★　　★　　★　　★　　★

Culture Note

You may want to point out that safety rules and safety equipment protect workers. Also, during inspections by government agencies, companies can be penalized or even closed if workers are not following safety regulations.

Careful　　　Quiet　　　Work Zone

1. Practice the dialog.

A　Monica! Be careful! Put on your goggles!
B　Oh, I'm sorry.

2. Work with a partner.

Circle CAREFUL, careful, quiet **and** QUIET.
Say the words.

WET FLOOR.
BE CAREFUL

Testing:
Please
be quiet.

Be careful.
Wet paint.

BE QUIET

68　　　　　　　　　　　　　　　　　　Unit 6

PREPARATION

Preteach the new language in the lesson. Follow these suggestions.

● Use picture cards, word cards, and pantomime to review the words **careful, quiet,** and **work zone.** See "Presenting Recognition Words" on page viii.

● Show a picture or have the group look at a work site. Point out possible hazards such as sharp objects or tools, electrical cords and outlets, hot objects, poisonous materials, and appliances.

● Preteach the dialog. To preteach **Be careful,** show a picture of a person in a dangerous situation. Say, *This is (Mohamed). (Mohamed), be careful!* Have learners repeat. Next, show a pair of goggles or a picture of them. Demonstrate the action and model *Put*

on your goggles! Have learners repeat and pantomime the action.

PRESENTATION

1. Focus attention on the illustration. Have learners say as much as they can about it. You may wish to point out items and have learners say the names, or say the names of items and have learners point them out. Restate their ideas in acceptable English and write them on the board or overhead projector.

Present the dialog. See "Presenting Dialogs" on page viii.

2. Help learners read the directions. Demonstrate by completing the first item on the board or overhead projector. Then have learners complete

the exercise. Check learners' work. Ask volunteers to read the words to the class.

3. Present or review the letters **q** and **z.** See "Presenting Letters" on page ix. Then have learners complete the exercise. Check learners' work. For extra reinforcement, use Blackline Master 3: Alphabet N-Z and Blackline Master 5: Lined Paper.

Environmental Print: Have learners point out examples of words with the letters **Q, q, Z,** and **z** in items they see in the room. For more information, see "Environmental Print" on page ix.

4. Help learners read the directions and the words in the box. Then have learners complete the exercise in pairs. Check learners' work. Then have learners say the words to a partner.

3. Write.

Write the letters. Say the letters. Say the words.

Q q

Q q

Z z

Z z

Q UIET	____ UIET	q uiet	____ uiet
Z ONE	____ ONE	z one	____ one
q uiet	____ uiet	z one	____ one

4. Write.

Write the words. Say the words.

careful   Zone

a. Work _Zone_   **b.** Be _careful_ .

Unit 6   69

FOLLOW-UP

Safety Equipment: Bring in pictures or realia of safety equipment such as goggles, gloves, a hard hat, and work boots. If possible, include safety equipment used at learners' workplaces or at places where they would like to work. Help learners say the names of the equipment. Supply the names for any other safety equipment that learners want to know.

♦ Have learners list the types of safety equipment that they use or see at work. Help learners record the words in their books or notebooks. Learners can illustrate their lists by drawing pictures for each of the words in their books or notebooks.

WORKFORCE SKILLS (pages 70-71)

Use public transportation to get to work

★   ★   ★   ★   ★

Walk   Drive   Take

1. Practice the dialog.

A George, do you take the bus to work?
B Yes, I take the 57 bus.

2. Work with a partner.

Circle WALK, drive, **and** Take. **Say the words.**

DON'T
WALK

Take the Train
15 minutes to
downtown

Please
drive
carefully.

3. Listen.

Circle the word you hear.

a. walk   drive   (take)   b. (walk)   drive   take

c. walk   (drive)   take   d. walk   drive   (take)

e. walk   (drive)   take   f. (walk)   drive   take

70   Unit 6

Language Note

As needed, introduce the names of other forms of transportation that are used in your area, such as trains and subways.

PREPARATION

Preteach the new language in the lesson. Follow these suggestions.

● Use picture cards, word cards, pantomime, and the illustrations in the book to preteach the recognition words **walk, drive,** and **take (the bus).** See "Presenting Recognition Words" on page viii.

● Preteach the dialog. Introduce the question, *Do you (take the bus) to work?* Have learners repeat and then respond to the question. Repeat the procedure using *walk* and *drive.*

PRESENTATION

 1. Focus attention on the illustration. Have learners say as much as they can about it. You may want to cue them by indicating the items and having learners say the names, or by saying names of items and having learners indicate them. Restate their ideas in acceptable English and write them on the board or overhead projector.

Present the dialog. See "Presenting Dialogs" on page viii.

2. Help learners read the directions. Demonstrate by completing the first item on the board or overhead projector. Then have learners complete the exercise in pairs. Check the exercise on the board or overhead projector. Have volunteers read the words aloud.

 3. Help learners read the directions. Then present the listening activity. See "Presenting Listening Activities" on page ix. Check learners' work. Ask volunteers to read their answers aloud.

4. Present or review the letters k and **b.** See "Presenting Letters" on page ix. Then have learners complete the exercise. Check learners' work. For extra reinforcement, use Blackline Master 2: Alphabet A-M, and Blackline Master 5: Lined Paper.

Environmental Print: Have learners point out examples of words with the letters **K, k, B,** and **b** in items they see in the room. For more information, see "Environmental Print" on page ix.

5. Help learners read the directions. Demonstrate by completing the first item on the board or overhead projector. Then have learners complete the exercise in pairs. Check learners'

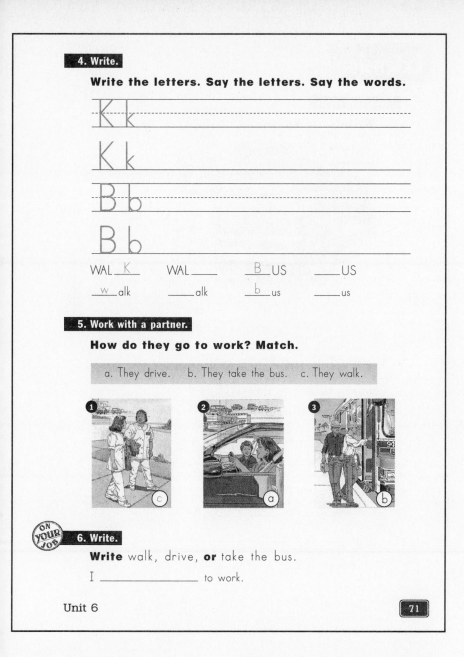

4. Write.

Write the letters. Say the letters. Say the words.

K k

K k

B b

B b

WAL _K_   WAL ___   _B_ US   ___US
_w_ alk   ___alk   _b_ us   ___us

5. Work with a partner.

How do they go to work? Match.

a. They drive.   b. They take the bus.   c. They walk.

1 — c   2 — a   3 — b

6. Write.

Write walk, drive, **or** take the bus.

I _____ to work.

work. Then ask volunteers to say the sentences aloud.

6. Help learners read the directions. Complete the item about yourself on the board or overhead projector. Have learners complete the activity. Check learners' work. Then ask volunteers to read their answers aloud.

FOLLOW-UP

Types of Transportation: Have learners brainstorm as many types of transportation as they can think of. Then ask pairs of learners to describe various places they might go on the different modes of transport listed. Have volunteers share their ideas with the class.

♦ Help learners name signs associated with each mode of transportation, such as **Bus Stop, Railroad Crossing, Speed Limit,** etc.

Read and write.

Write early **or** late.

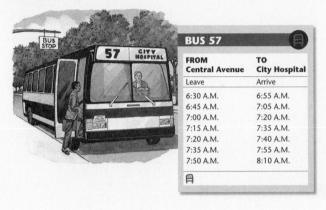

BUS 57	
FROM **Central Avenue**	**TO** **City Hospital**
Leave	Arrive
6:30 A.M.	6:55 A.M.
6:45 A.M.	7:05 A.M.
7:00 A.M.	7:20 A.M.
7:15 A.M.	7:35 A.M.
7:20 A.M.	7:40 A.M.
7:35 A.M.	7:55 A.M.
7:50 A.M.	8:10 A.M.

First shift at City Hospital starts at 7:30.

a. Pablo is taking the bus at 7:00.

He's going to be ___early___ for work.

b. Amy is taking the bus at 7:20.

She's going to be ___late___ for work.

c. Stan is taking the bus at 6:45.

He's going to be ___early___ for work.

d. Ji Sun is taking the bus at 7:15.

She's going to be ___late___ for work.

`72`

Unit 6

PREPARATION

Review the new language using the following suggestions.

● Provide learners with copies of Blackline Master 11: Clock. Say, *Work starts at 8:00.* Ask learners to set the time on their clocks. Check learners' work. Then draw a person and show a clock with the time 8:30. Ask another volunteer to tell what time the person is arriving. Hold up word cards for **early** and **late.** Ask volunteers to read the words and decide if the person is early or late. Repeat with another person and the time 7:45.

PRESENTATION

Help learners read the directions. Focus attention on the illustrations. Ask learners to say as much as they can about

them. Restate learners' ideas in acceptable English and write them on the board or overhead projector. Help learners read the times and places on the bus schedule. You may want to ask questions to make sure learners understand the schedule. Help learners read the introductory line under the illustrations. Write the first item on the board or overhead projector. Demonstrate the activity by reading the sentences in the first item aloud and filling in the missing word. Have learners complete the activity in pairs. Check learners' work. Have volunteers read their answers aloud.

FOLLOW-UP

Bus Routes and Schedules: Bring in a bus map and schedule for a local bus route. Help learners look over the map

and identify the places and read the street names. Ask learners about the bus schedule. Say, *You're at (Walnut Street). What time is the next bus to (the mall)?*

♦ In small groups, have learners find the bus stops closest to their work and/or school. Ask learners to find out when the bus stops near these places.

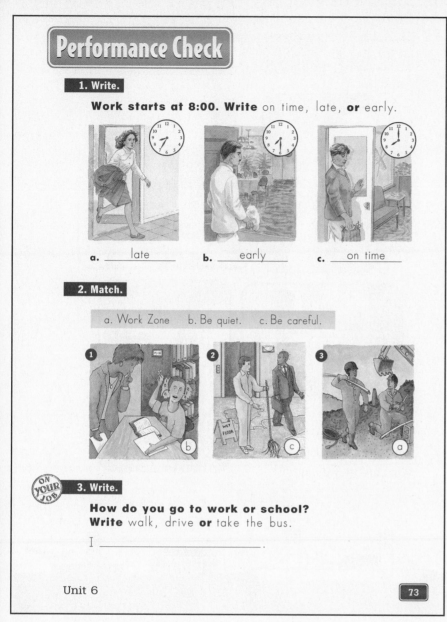

Performance Check

1. Write.

Work starts at 8:00. Write on time, late, **or** early.

a. ___late___ b. ___early___ c. ___on time___

2. Match.

a. Work Zone   b. Be quiet.   c. Be careful.

3. Write.

How do you go to work or school?
Write walk, drive **or** take the bus.

I _____ .

Unit 6

73

ASAP PROJECT

Help learners compile a class book of common workplace rules. Learners may use rules from their own workplaces or from their Student Book. Have each learner choose a rule and submit a page about it. Learners can draw or cut out a magazine picture to illustrate the rule or to show the importance of the rule. They should also write the rule.

Help learners arrange the rules in the book in a logical sequence and prepare a table of contents. Make a copy of the rule book for each class member.

PREPARATION

Briefly review the new language before learners open their books. Follow these suggestions.

● Write the words **on time, early,** and **late** on the board or overhead projector. Write the time that work starts. Then show a clock with various times before, after, and exactly on the start time. Ask volunteers to say the recognition words that apply to each of the times.

● Show the word cards for **quiet, careful,** and **work zone.** Ask volunteers to mime actions associated with the recognition words.

● Write the words **walk, drive,** and **take the bus** on the board or overhead projector. Ask volunteers to find the

matching picture cards or to indicate appropriate illustrations in their books.

Provide specific help as needed until you are sure learners feel confident that they know all the new words.

PRESENTATION

Use any of the procedures in "Evaluation," page ix, with this page. Record each individual's results on the Unit 6 Individual Competency Chart. Record the class's results on the Class Cumulative Competency Chart.

INFORMAL WORKPLACE-SPECIFIC ASSESSMENT

Ask learners to identify the person and phone number that they must call if they will be absent or late.

Unit 7 Overview

—SCANS Competencies—

★ Interpret and communicate information

★ Serve clients and customers

★ Acquire and evaluate information

Unit 7 Workforce Skills

- Understand amounts of money
- Count money and make change
- Write a check
- Cash one's paycheck
- Make a deposit

Materials

- Number cards and word cards for **1** through **20, 30, 40, 50, 60, 70, 80,** and **90**
- Realia, pictures, and word cards for coins and currency
- Realia, picture cards, and word cards for **dollar, cents, change, cash, check, paycheck, ID, deposit,** and the symbol **$**
- Realia or pictures of shoes, a tool-box, gloves, a telephone, a lamp, a camera, a personal radio, a television, a vacuum cleaner, a washing machine, and a notebook
- Realia: calculators or adding machines and deposit slips
- Blackline Master 12: Money and Blackline Master 13: Blank Check and Deposit Slip

★   ★   ★   ★   ★

UNIT 7 **Finances**

Look at the pictures.

Where are the people?

What are they doing?

Unit 7

WORKFORCE SKILLS (page 74)

Talk about money

★   ★   ★   ★   ★

Teaching Note

Use Blackline Masters 6 and 7: Common Directions to clarify the directions in this unit. Use page 74 to warm up learners, to check on prior knowledge, and to spark interest.

PREPARATION

Begin the class by showing real money or pictures of money. Help learners name places where money is used. Ask learners to discuss what they buy.

PRESENTATION

Focus attention on the illustrations. Have learners say as much as they can about them. Learners may be able to name a few items in the pictures, but you may have to prompt them by naming items and having learners repeat. You also might read the questions aloud for learners to answer. Clarify any words learners do not know.

You might mention the places shown and the ways people use money and checks.

FOLLOW-UP

What Do You Do With Your Money?

Provide pairs of learners with magazines. Ask learners to cut out pictures of things they buy or of ways they use their money.

Have each pair of learners show their pictures to the class and identify the items or actions. Encourage them to tell where and why they buy or use these things. Provide feedback as necessary.

♦ Have pairs of learners make groups of four. Ask each pair to show their pictures to the other pair and identify the items or actions. Create a four-column chart on a large sheet of paper for each group. Have learners write their names at the tops of the columns and then tape or glue their pictures in the columns. Encourage learners to compare and contrast the different items and actions. Help learners summarize the chart. Are there some things that everyone buys?

English ASAP

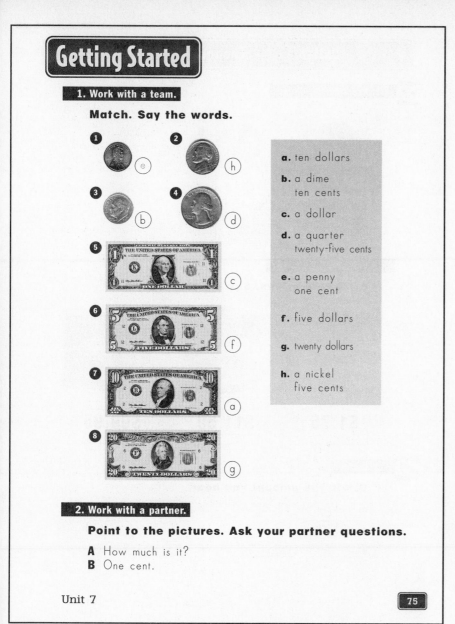

Getting Started

1. Work with a team.

Match. Say the words.

1 ③ e
2 ④ h
3 ⑤ b
4 ⑥ d
5 ⑦ c
6 ⑧ f
7 ⑨ a
8 ⑩ g

a. ten dollars

b. a dime
   ten cents

c. a dollar

d. a quarter
   twenty-five cents

e. a penny
   one cent

f. five dollars

g. twenty dollars

h. a nickel
   five cents

2. Work with a partner.

Point to the pictures. Ask your partner questions.

A How much is it?
B One cent.

Unit 7   75

Teaching Note

Use this page to introduce the new language in the unit. Whenever possible, encourage peer teaching. Supply any language the learners need.

PREPARATION

Use number cards to review numbers **1** through **20.** Then present the word cards for the numbers **1** through **20.** Help learners match the number and word cards.

Preteach the new words in the lesson. Follow these suggestions.

● To teach the words **penny, nickel, dime, quarter, dollar,** and **cents,** use real coins and bills or Blackline Master 12: Money. Focus attention on each coin or bill, identify it, and have learners repeat.

● To teach **How much is it?** hold up some one-dollar bills or play money and say, *How much is it? One dollar? Two dollars? Three dollars?* Show learners the corresponding number of bills. Then have a volunteer count the money and say the amount.

PRESENTATION

1. Focus attention on the illustrations. Have learners say as much as they can about them. Then help learners read the directions. Demonstrate by completing the first item on the board or overhead projector. Have learners complete the activity in teams. Encourage learners to work together. Go over the answers with the class.

2. Help learners read the directions. Model the dialog as learners listen. Say the dialog again and have learners repeat. Ask learners to practice the dialog with a partner. Then model substituting the next item on the page in the dialog, and ask learners to continue similarly with the remaining items.

FOLLOW-UP

How Much Is It? Make sets of cards with pictures of the coins and bills or use Blackline Master 12: Money. Make other sets with the words for the coins and bills and/or amounts. Give groups of learners a set of picture cards and a set of word cards. Learners can match the items. Have a volunteer in each group ask the others to find and give him or her the various coins and bills.

♦ Arrange a pile of coins and play money on a table. Ask volunteers to come and find the correct coin or bill or combination that you request. For example: *Show me twenty-five cents./Show me two quarters./Show me five dollars.*

Understand amounts of money

Count money and make change

★ ★ ★ ★ ★

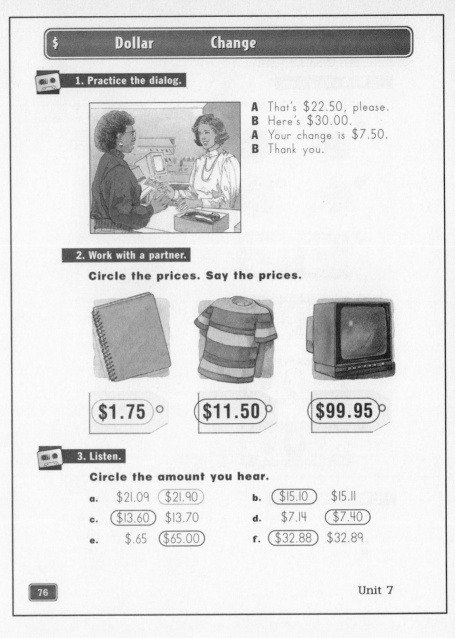

$ Dollar Change

1. Practice the dialog.

A That's $22.50, please.
B Here's $30.00.
A Your change is $7.50.
B Thank you.

2. Work with a partner.

Circle the prices. Say the prices.

$1.75 $11.50 $99.95

3. Listen.

Circle the amount you hear.

a. $21.09   ($21.90)   b. ($15.10) $15.11
c. ($13.60) $13.70   d. $7.14   ($7.40)
e. $.65   ($65.00)   f. ($32.88) $32.89

76   Unit 7

Language Note

*In this lesson, **change** refers to the money returned when more than enough money is used to pay for an item.*

PREPARATION

Preteach the new language in the lesson. Follow these suggestions.

● Use word cards, real bills, coins, or Blackline Master 12: Money to preteach the recognition words **dollar, change,** and the symbol **$**. See "Presenting Recognition Words" on page viii.

● Say amounts aloud and have learners repeat. Write the amounts on the board and have learners say them. Show coins in various combinations and say and write the totals. Repeat with bills. Then write prices on the board or overhead projector and have learners count out the amounts in play money.

● Write prices on the board or overhead projector. Act out paying with a bill

larger than the price. Model counting out the change. Write other prices, show bills used for payment, and have learners determine the amount of change.

● Preteach the dialog. Point to the worker in the illustration. Pantomime requesting payment. Say, *That's $23.00, please.* Model the request and have learners repeat. Then display $30.00 and model the response, *Here's $30.00.* Have learners repeat. Pantomime counting and giving the change to the customer. Say, *Your change is $7.00.* Have learners repeat.

PRESENTATION

 1. Focus attention on the illustration. Help learners identify the place, the worker, and the customer. Have them say as much as

they can about the illustration. You may want to cue them by indicating the items and having learners say the names, or by saying names of items and having learners indicate them. Restate learners' ideas in acceptable English and write them on the board or overhead projector.

Present the dialog. See "Presenting Dialogs" on page viii.

2. Help learners read the directions. Demonstrate by circling the price of the first item and then reading aloud the amount. Then have learners complete the exercise in pairs. Ask volunteers to read aloud the prices.

 3. Help learners read the directions. Then present the listening activity. See "Presenting Listening Activities" on

4. Write.

Write the amounts. Say the amounts.

a. $12.35

b. $25.12

c. $2.90

5. Work with a partner.

Write the change.

○ **$12.00**　　○ **$1.25**　　○ **$10.50**

a. $3.00

b. $.75

c. $9.50

6. Work with a partner.

Practice the dialog. Use the prices from 5.

A That's ___$12.00___, please.

B Here's ___$15.00___.

A Your change is ___$3.00___.

B Thank you.

Unit 7

 77

Language Note

Clarify that an amount of money can be said in various ways. For example, $5.75 can be said **five dollars and seventy-five cents** *or* **five seventy-five.**

page ix. Check learners' work. Ask volunteers to read their answers aloud.

4. Help learners read the directions. Demonstrate by completing the first item on the board or overhead projector. Have learners complete the exercise independently. Check the exercise on the board or overhead projector. Then have learners read the amounts aloud.

5. Help learners read the directions. Demonstrate by completing the first item on the board or overhead projector. Have learners complete the exercise with a partner. You might have learners use play money to figure out the correct change. Ask several learners to read their answers aloud.

6. Help learners read the directions. Review the dialog with the class. Then have learners practice the dialog in pairs, switching partners and changing roles several times using the amounts from 5. Have several pairs say the dialog aloud for the class.

FOLLOW-UP

Your Change Is: Provide each learner with a picture of an item or a real item such as a notebook, gloves, etc. Ask the learner to write a price for the item. (You may also help learners talk about items they use for their own jobs. Model any words learners do not know.) Then arrange learners in pairs with play money or copies of money from Blackline Master 12: Money. Learners pay their partners for the items with an amount greater than the price. The partners provide change as needed.

♦ If possible, distribute calculators or adding machines to groups of learners. Model using a calculator or adding machine to calculate change. Say other examples of money paid and the purchase price. Learners can use the calculators to determine the amount of change.

Understand amounts of money

Write a check

★   ★   ★   ★   ★

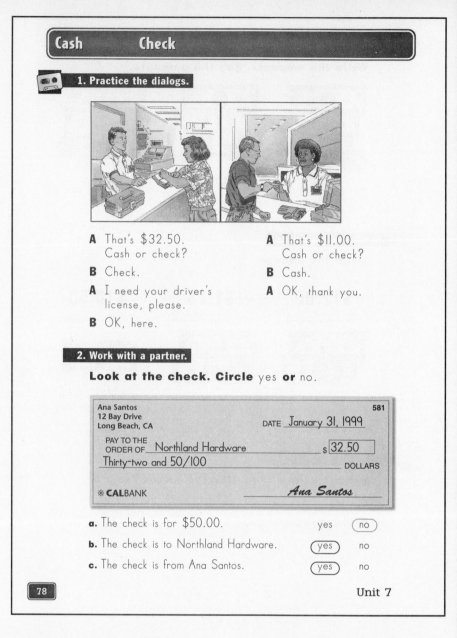

Cash   Check

 1. Practice the dialogs.

A That's $32.50.
Cash or check?

B Check.

A I need your driver's
license, please.

B OK, here.

A That's $11.00.
Cash or check?

B Cash.

A OK, thank you.

2. Work with a partner.

Look at the check. Circle yes **or** no.

```
Ana Santos                                            581
12 Bay Drive
Long Beach, CA              DATE January 31, 1999
    PAY TO THE
    ORDER OF  Northland Hardware        $ 32.50
Thirty-two and 50/100 _____ DOLLARS

✳ CALBANK                       Ana Santos
```

a. The check is for $50.00.   yes   (no)

b. The check is to Northland Hardware.   (yes)   no

c. The check is from Ana Santos.   (yes)   no

78   Unit 7

Teaching Note

You may wish to teach learners to write numbers in words over the course of several days rather than in one lesson.

PREPARATION

Preteach the new language in the lesson. Follow these suggestions.

● To teach the concept of a check, show learners a real check or the blank check from Blackline Master 13: Blank Check and Deposit Slip. Explain that people can use checks instead of cash to pay for things, that checks come from banks, and that checks represent money in the bank.

● Use real items and word cards to preteach the recognition words **cash** and **check.** See "Presenting Recognition Words" on page viii.

● Explain that the dollar amounts on a check are written in both numbers and words. Then teach or review numbers **1** through **100** in words. Write a numeral

on the board or overhead projector, have a learner read it aloud, and write the word for the number on the board or overhead projector.

● Preteach the dialogs. To teach the line *I need your driver's license,* pantomime giving a salesclerk your license. Explain that the salesclerk needs to make sure that the person writing the check is the person whose name is on the check.

PRESENTATION

 1. Focus attention on the illustration. Help learners identify the place, the people, and the items. Have them say as much as they can about the illustration. You may want to cue them by indicating the items for them to name or by saying names of

items and having learners indicate them. Restate their ideas in acceptable English and write them on the board or overhead projector.

Present the dialogs. See "Presenting Dialogs" on page viii.

2. Help learners read the directions. Point out how much the check is for and to whom it is written. Help learners read the statements. Demonstrate by circling the answer to the first item on the board or overhead projector. Then have them complete the exercise in pairs. Check the exercise on the board or overhead projector.

3. Help learners read the directions. Then present the listening activity. See "Presenting Listening Activities" on

3. Listen.

Write cash **or** check.

a. _____cash_____   b. _____check_____

c. _____cash_____   d. _____check_____

4. Match.

Match the amounts.

__c__ **1.** $15.95   **a.** Twenty-one and 50/100 DOLLARS

__a__ **2.** $21.50   **b.** Sixty-two and 75/100 DOLLARS

__b__ **3.** $62.75   **c.** Fifteen and 95/100 DOLLARS

5. Write.

Write the amounts for checks.

$40.20 _____Forty and 20/100_____ Dollars

$71.05 _____Seventy-one and 05/100_____ Dollars

$65.30 _____Sixty-five and 30/100_____ Dollars

6. Write.

Write a check to Northland Hardware for $34.78.

```
                                                    226
              DATE _____

PAY TO THE
ORDER OF  Northland Hardware          $ | 34.78 |

 Thirty-four and 78/100 _____  DOLLARS


✳CALBANK                 _____
```

Unit 7   **79**

---

page ix. Check learners' work. Ask volunteers to read their answers aloud.

4. Help learners read the directions. Demonstrate by completing the first item on the board or overhead projector. Then have learners complete the exercise independently. Check learners' work. Ask volunteers to say their answers aloud.

5. Help learners read the directions. Demonstrate by completing the first item on the board or overhead projector. Then ask learners to complete the exercise independently. Check learners' work. Ask volunteers to say their answers aloud.

6. Help learners read the directions. Draw a check on the board or overhead projector and demonstrate filling it in. Then have learners complete the exercise independently. Check learners' work. Ask a different volunteer to fill in each part of the check on the board or overhead projector.

FOLLOW-UP

Paying by Check: Provide learners with multiple copies of blank checks using Blackline Master 13: Blank Check and Deposit Slip. Ask learners what they might pay for by check (rent, gas, phone, etc.) and appropriate amounts they might pay. Help learners

brainstorm. Write local utility and business names and money amounts on the board or overhead projector so learners can refer to them. Then have them work in pairs to write checks to these businesses.

♦ Have learners write additional checks for other items or bills they want to pay by check.

WORKFORCE SKILLS (pages 80-81)

Cash one's paycheck

★   ★   ★   ★   ★

Language Note

*Explain to learners that **endorsing a
check** means signing the back of a check.*

Paycheck   ID   Sign

1. Practice the dialog.

ENDORSE HERE
Hector Perez

DO NOT WRITE OR SIGN BELOW THIS LINE

A Hello, I want to cash my paycheck.
B I need some ID, please.
A Here's my driver's license.
B Thank you. Sign your name here.

2. Work with a partner.

What is it? Circle the words. Say the words.

Green Tree Co.
23 South Street
Boston, MA 02111   48295

Pay to the
order of   Arturo Morales $ 400.00
Four hundred and no/100 dollars

                                Bill Perkins

Driver's License
12897654
Arturo Morales
12 Third Street
Boston, MA 02125
DOB: 05-05-58

a. (paycheck)   ID   **b.**   cash   (ID)

Unit 7

PREPARATION

Preteach the new language in the lesson.
Follow these suggestions.

● Use real examples of paychecks
and ID (a driver's license), word cards,
and pantomime to preteach the words
paycheck, ID, and **sign.** See "Presenting
Recognition Words" on page viii.

● Preteach the dialog. Model the
expression *I want to cash my paycheck.*
Explain that to cash a check means to
receive the amount in money. Have
learners repeat the sentence. Then say,
Sign your name here and demonstrate
signing your name. Have learners repeat
and sign their own names.

PRESENTATION

 1. Focus attention on the illustrations. Have learners say as
much as they can about them.
You may want to cue them by indicating the items for learners to name, or by
saying names of items and having learners indicate them. Restate their ideas in
acceptable English and write them on
the board or overhead projector.

Present the dialog. See "Presenting
Dialogs" on page viii.

2. Help learners read the directions.
Demonstrate by completing the first
item on the board or overhead projector.
Then have learners complete the exercise. Ask volunteers to read the answers
to the class.

 3. Help learners read the
directions. Then present
the listening activity. See
"Presenting Listening Activities" on
page ix. Check learners' work. Ask
volunteers to read their answers aloud.

4. Help learners read the directions.
Point out how much the check is for,
to whom it is written, and when it was
written. Help learners read the questions. Demonstrate by writing the
answer to the first item on the board or
overhead projector. Then have learners
complete the exercise independently.
Check learners' work. Ask volunteers
to write the answers on the board or
overhead projector.

---

3. Listen.

Do they ask for ID? Circle yes **or** no.

a. (yes)   no   b.   yes   (no)

c.   yes   (no)   d. (yes)   no

4. Read and write.

Read the paycheck. Write the answers.

Medical Labs
44 Sky Avenue
Chicago, IL 60609

DATE _June 1, 2000_

PAY TO THE ORDER OF _____ MEI CHIN _____

THREE HUNDRED TWENTY-FIVE AND 14/100 DOLLARS $ | 325.14 |

✦**National** Bank   _Ellen Martinka_

---

a. Who is the check for? _____ Mei Chin _____

b. What is the amount of the check? _____ $325.14 _____

c. What is the date of the check? _____ June 1, 2000 _____

5. Write.

Sign the backs of the checks.

ENDORSE HERE

_____

_____

DO NOT WRITE OR SIGN BELOW THIS LINE

ENDORSE HERE

_____

_____

DO NOT WRITE OR SIGN BELOW THIS LINE

Unit 7   81

Teaching Note

Use Blackline Master 13: Blank Check and Deposit Slip for additional practice for signing names. If necessary, write learners' names in cursive on their papers and have them copy and develop their own signatures.

5. Help learners read the directions. Demonstrate by signing your name on the board or overhead projector. Then ask learners to complete the exercise independently. Check learners' work.

FOLLOW-UP

Cashing Checks: Use Blackline Master 13: Blank Check and Deposit Slip to provide each learner with a blank check. Arrange learners in pairs and instruct each learner to write a check to his or her partner for any amount under $100 and then give the check to his or her partner. Ask learners to endorse the checks they received. Check to make sure learners have endorsed their checks correctly.

◆ Ask a volunteer to play the role of a bank teller. Have learners come forward to the "bank" one at a time and exchange their endorsed checks for bills and coins. Use Blackline Master 12: Money. Suggest that learners count the money they receive to verify that it is the correct amount. Then have other learners check the amounts.

WORKFORCE SKILLS (pages 82-83)

Make a deposit

★   ★   ★   ★   ★

Language Note

Explain that deposit slips may have **Deposit, Deposit Slip,** *or* **Deposit Ticket** *printed on them, but* **deposit slip** *is more commonly used in spoken English.*

Deposit

1. Practice the dialog.

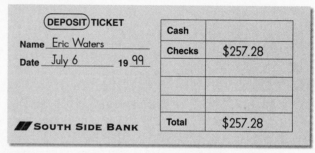

A Hello, I want to deposit this check.
B OK, please fill out a deposit slip.
A Thank you.

2. Circle.

Circle DEPOSIT. **Circle** yes **or** no.

(DEPOSIT) TICKET	Cash	
Name Eric Waters	Checks	$257.28
Date July 6 19 99		
///SOUTH SIDE BANK	Total	$257.28

a. Eric is depositing his check. (yes)   no

b. The check is for $275.80.   yes   (no)

c. The date is July 6.   (yes)   no

d. Eric's bank is North Bank.   yes   (no)

82

Unit 7

PREPARATION

Preteach the new language in the lesson. Follow these suggestions.

● To teach the concept of a deposit, show learners a real check and a deposit slip. Explain that people can cash checks or put (deposit) the money in the bank for later use.

● Use Blackline Master 13: Blank Check and Deposit Slip and the word card to preteach the recognition word **deposit.** See "Presenting Recognition Words" on page viii.

● Preteach the dialog. Show a check and model the sentence *I want to deposit this check.* Have learners repeat the sentence. Then show a deposit slip and say, *Please fill out a deposit slip.* Ask learners to repeat. Pantomime filling out the slip.

PRESENTATION

1. Focus attention on the illustration. Have learners say as much as they can about it. You may want to cue them by indicating the items for learners to name or by saying names of items and having learners indicate them. Restate their ideas in acceptable English and write them on the board or overhead projector.

Present the dialog. See "Presenting Dialogs" on page viii.

2. Help learners read the directions. Point out the amount of the deposit, the name of the person depositing the money, the name of the bank, and the date. Help learners read the statements. Demonstrate by circling the answer to the first item on the board or overhead projector. Then have learners complete the exercise

independently. Check learners' work. Ask volunteers to write the answers on the board or overhead projector.

3. Help learners read the directions. Then present the listening activity. See "Presenting Listening Activities" on page ix. Check learners' work. Ask volunteers to read their answers aloud.

4. Help learners read the directions. Point out the amount of the check. Remind learners to use their own names and the current date on the deposit slip. Draw a deposit slip on the board or overhead projector. Demonstrate by filling in your name on the deposit slip on the board or overhead projector. Then have learners complete the exercise independently. Check learners' work.

3. Listen.

Do you hear deposit? **Circle** yes **or** no.

a. (yes)   no   b. (yes)   no

c. yes   (no)   d. (yes)   no

e. (yes)   no   f.   yes   (no)

4. Write.

You have a check for $251.77. Deposit it.

DEPOSIT TICKET

Name _____

Address _____

_____

Date _____

SIGN HERE

_____

≋ *Trust Bank*

CASH	
CHECKS	$251.77
TOTAL	$251.77

5. Write.

You have a check for $361.21. Deposit it.

DEPOSIT TICKET

Name _____

Address _____

_____

Date _____

SIGN HERE

West Bank

CASH	
CHECKS	$361.21
TOTAL	$361.21

Unit 7

83

5. Follow the same procedure as in 4.

FOLLOW-UP

At the Bank: Take learners to visit a local bank. You may wish to call the bank first. Show learners where to find deposit slips and information on bank accounts. (If it is not possible to visit a bank, bring in, or have learners bring in, deposit slips from several banks.) When you return to the class, have learners compare the bank deposit slips to the ones in the book. Help them point out similarities and differences between the forms. Learners can practice filling out one of the bank deposit slips with the information from activity 4 or 5.

♦ Make copies of blank deposit slips or use blank deposit slips from the bank. Point out places for filling in cash amounts and checks. Write on the board combinations of cash and checks. Tell learners to fill out deposit slips for the combinations. Learners can work in pairs and use calculators to total the amounts deposited.

The Extension page shows:

Extension

1. Circle.

Circle the item you want.

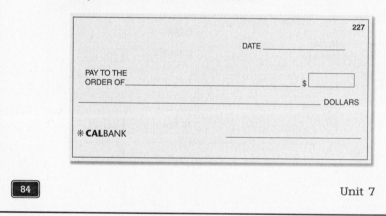

Dart Discount

Vacuum Cleaner $112.99

Television $129.99

Telephone $32.95

Camera $89.90

Personal Radio $12.45

Lamp $19.50

Washer $199.95

2. Write.

Buy the item. Write a check.

227

DATE _____

PAY TO THE ORDER OF _____ $ _____

_____ DOLLARS

✳ **CAL**BANK _____

84

Unit 7

PREPARATION

Review the new language using the following suggestions.

• If necessary, review numbers using the procedure on page 78.

• On the board or overhead projector, write the words **dollars** and **check.** Ask volunteers to read the words aloud and find a matching illustration in the book for each.

• Use copies of Blackline Master 13: Blank Check and Deposit Slip to review writing checks.

PRESENTATION

Help learners read the directions. Focus attention on the illustration and ask learners to say as much about it as they can. Model any words learners want to know. Demonstrate by choosing an item you wish to buy and filling out a blank check for the correct amount on the board or overhead projector. Then have learners complete the exercise independently. Check learners' work. Encourage learners to share their choices with the class. Ask volunteers to show their checks to the rest of the class.

FOLLOW-UP

Store Flyers: Provide pairs with flyers or advertisements from local stores. Distribute copies of blank checks. Have learners choose an item from the flyer to purchase and write a check for the total amount.

♦ Have learners choose two or three items from the flyer or advertisement. Learners can add up the prices of the articles they want to buy and then fill out a check for the total.

1. Write.

Write the amounts.

a. ___$4.85___　　b. ___$16.25___　　c. ___$22.20___

2. Write.

Write a check to Green's Grocery for $40.82.

		375
	DATE _____	
PAY TO THE ORDER OF _Green's Grocery_	$	40.82
Forty and 82/100 _____		DOLLARS
✳ **CAL**BANK	_____	

3. Listen.

Circle the amount you hear.

a. ⟨$27.98⟩　$27.99　　　b. $4.80　⟨$48.00⟩

c. $14.01　⟨$14.10⟩　　　d. $15.55　⟨$55.15⟩

e. ⟨$30.25⟩　$30.52　　　f. ⟨$11.11⟩　$1.11

Unit 7　　　　　　　　　　　　　　　　　　85

ASAP
PROJECT

You may want to help learners set up a simple store in the classroom and role-play shopping for office supplies or work-related supplies. For merchandise, use picture cards and pictures from catalogs and circulars spread out on desks and/or tables. Help learners decide on a type of store and arrange pictures in logical groupings. Have them attach price tags to each item. Some learners can be customers and others, store clerks. Learners can use blank checks and play money to make transactions. Use Blackline Master 12: Money and Blackline Master 13: Blank Check and Deposit Slip. Remind store clerks to check ID when accepting checks for payment.

Set aside some time after the role play for learners to discuss what they learned in setting up the store and taking the roles of customers and clerks.

PREPARATION

Briefly review the new language before learners open their books. Follow these suggestions.

● Review amounts of money and how to write a check using realia, word cards, and picture cards.

● Review the spelling of number words using number and word cards.

● Say sentences with money amounts. Have learners write the amounts.

Provide specific help as needed until you are sure learners feel confident that they know all the new words and language.

PRESENTATION

Use any of the procedures in "Evaluation," page ix, with this page. Record individuals' results on the Unit 7 Individual Competency Chart. Record the class's results on the Class Cumulative Competency Chart.

INFORMAL WORKPLACE-SPECIFIC ASSESSMENT

Have learners fill out a deposit slip for a check of their own.

Unit 7　　　　　　　　　　　　　　　　　　　　　　　　　　85

Unit 8 Overview

—SCANS Competencies—

★ Acquire and evaluate information

★ Understand technological systems

★ Interpret and communicate
  information

Unit 8 Workforce Skills

- Identify parts of the body
- State symptoms and injuries
- Read safety signs
- Call 911
- Identify unsafe working conditions
- Follow safety instructions

Materials

- Picture cards and word cards for parts
  of the body: **arm, hand, foot, leg,
  back,** and **eye**
- Picture cards and word cards for
  injuries and places for medical help:
  hurt, cut, broken, hospital, and
  emergency room
- Word cards for signs and emergencies: **Danger, No Smoking, Poison,
  fire, 911,** and **accident**
- A picture of a fire truck
- Realia: a first-aid kit
- Blackline Master 5: Lined Paper and
  Blackline Master 10: Telephone

★　　★　　★　　★　　★

UNIT **8** | **Health and Safety**

Look at the pictures.

Where are the people?

What are they doing?

86

Unit 8

WORKFORCE SKILLS (page 86)

Identify parts of the body

State symptoms and injuries

Read safety signs

Call 911

★　　★　　★　　★　　★

Teaching Note

*Use Blackline Masters 6 and 7: Common
Directions to clarify the directions in this
unit. Use page 86 to warm up learners,
to check and draw on prior knowledge,
and to spark interest.*

PRESENTATION

Focus attention on the illustrations.
Have learners say as much as they can
about them. Learners may be able to

name a few items in the pictures, but
you may have to prompt them by
naming the safety equipment, jobs,
signs, and health-related problems
pictured and have learners repeat. You
also might read the questions aloud for
learners to answer. Model any language
learners need.

FOLLOW-UP

Health Services: Ask learners to name
places that they or other people go for
help when they are sick or hurt. List on
the board or overhead projector the
places learners name and add important
clinics or hospitals they may have omit-
ted. Ask learners if they have ever gone
to any of the places. Have volunteers
share their experiences with the class.

♦ Help learners look up the telephone
numbers of the health facilities on the
list in a telephone directory. Write the
numbers on the board or overhead
projector. Give learners time to copy
the information they need.

Getting Started

1. Work with a team.

Match. Write the letter.

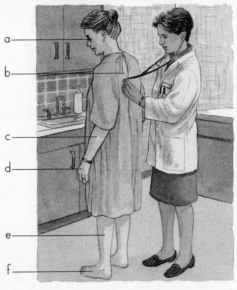

1. _c_ arm   2. _f_ foot
3. _b_ back   4. _d_ hand
5. _e_ leg   6. _a_ eye

2. Work with a partner.

Give your partner instructions.
Your partner points to the picture.

A Point to her arm.

Unit 8   `87`

Teaching Note

Use this page to introduce the new language in the unit. Whenever possible, encourage peer teaching. Supply any language the learners need.

Culture Note

In the activities in this unit, it may be more appropriate to gesture with your full hand rather than point, as some cultures consider pointing fingers at people to be offensive. Similarly, if you think learners will feel uncomfortable gesturing towards themselves in the activities in this unit, tell them to touch the picture on this page.

PREPARATION

Focus attention on the illustration. Have learners say as much as they can about it. Learners may be able to name a few items, but you may have to prompt them by naming items and having learners repeat. Help learners identify the parts of the body, the doctor, and the patient.

PRESENTATION

1. Help learners read the directions. Demonstrate by completing the first item on the board or overhead projector. Have learners complete the exercise in teams. Encourage learners to work together. Go over the answers with the class.

2. Help learners read the directions. Model the command as learners listen. Say the command again and have learners repeat. Ask learners to practice the first item with a partner. Then model substituting the next item on the page in the command, and ask learners to continue similarly with the remaining items.

FOLLOW-UP

Identifying Parts of the Body:
Have learners stand. Give a series of commands, such as *Touch your (foot)*. Demonstrate by giving the command and performing the action yourself. Then ask the class to perform the action as you say it, either by touching their feet or touching the picture on the Student Book page.

♦ One at a time, hold up word cards with the names of the parts of the body and ask each learner to touch that part of his or her body.

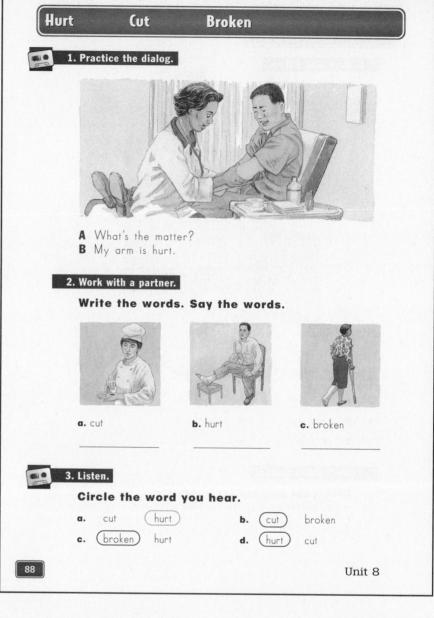

Hurt   Cut   Broken

1. Practice the dialog.

A What's the matter?
B My arm is hurt.

2. Work with a partner.

Write the words. Say the words.

a. cut   **b.** hurt   **c.** broken

_____   _____   _____

3. Listen.

Circle the word you hear.

a. cut   (hurt)   **b.** (cut)   broken

c. (broken)   hurt   **d.** (hurt)   cut

88   Unit 8

PREPARATION

Preteach the new language in the lesson. Follow these suggestions.

● Use pictures and word cards to review the parts of the body. See "Presenting Recognition Words" on page viii.

● Preteach the dialog. Pretend to hurt your arm. Hold your arm, grimace, and say, *My arm is hurt.* Have learners repeat. Then ask a volunteer to act out hurting his or her arm. Ask, *What's the matter?* Prompt the learner to answer, *My arm is hurt.*

PRESENTATION

 1. Focus attention on the illustration. Have learners say as much as they can about it. You may want to cue them by indicating the

place and people and having learners say the names, or by naming the place and people and having learners indicate them. Restate their ideas in acceptable English and write them on the board or overhead projector.

Present the dialog. See "Presenting Dialogs" on page viii.

2. Help learners read the directions. Demonstrate by reading the words aloud. Write the first word. Then have learners complete the exercise in pairs.

 3. Help learners read the directions. Then present the listening activity. See "Presenting Listening Activities" on page ix. Check learners' work. Ask volunteers to read their answers aloud.

4. Help learners read the directions. Demonstrate by completing the first item on the board or overhead projector. Have learners complete the exercise independently. Check learners' work. Then ask volunteers to read their answers aloud.

 5. Help learners read the directions. With learners, brainstorm possible answers and write them on the board or overhead projector. Then have learners complete the exercise. Check learners' work. Ask volunteers to read their answers aloud.

6. Help learners read the directions. Demonstrate with a volunteer. Then have learners practice the dialog. Have learners change partners and repeat the

4. Write.

Complete the sentences.

broken   cut   hurt   hurt

a. His back is _____ hurt _____ .   **b.** Her arm is _____ broken _____ .

c. Her leg is _____ cut _____ .   **d.** His foot is _____ hurt _____ .

5. Write.

You're hurt. Complete the dialog.

A What's the matter?

B My _____ is _____ .

6. Work with a partner.

Practice the dialog in 5.

Unit 8   89

exercise several times. Ask several pairs
to say their conversations for the class.

FOLLOW-UP

Injuries: Help learners brainstorm a list of
other injuries that might occur at learners'
workplaces, such as burns and sprains.
Write the words on the board or overhead
projector and help learners say them.

◆ Help learners list safety/first aid
items at their workplaces, such as first
aid kits, eyewash stations, and safety
showers. You may need to sketch them
on the board or pantomime them. Say
the words and have learners repeat.

Read safety signs

Identify unsafe working conditions

★ ★ ★ ★ ★

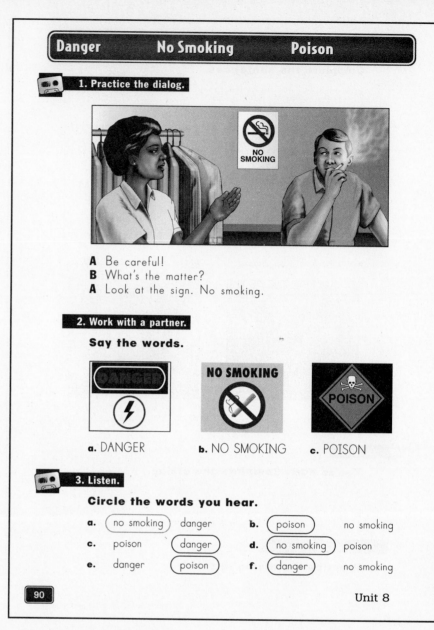

Danger   No Smoking   Poison

1. Practice the dialog.

A Be careful!
B What's the matter?
A Look at the sign. No smoking.

2. Work with a partner.

Say the words.

a. DANGER   b. NO SMOKING   c. POISON

3. Listen.

Circle the words you hear.

a. (no smoking) danger   b. (poison) no smoking
c. poison (danger)   d. (no smoking) poison
e. danger (poison)   f. (danger) no smoking

90   Unit 8

SCANS Note

Tell learners they should become familiar with their workplaces' safety rules whenever they start new jobs.

PREPARATION

Preteach the new language in the lesson. Follow these suggestions.

• Use word cards, pantomime, and explanation to preteach the recognition words **Danger, No Smoking,** and **Poison.** See "Presenting Recognition Words" on page viii.

• Preteach the dialog. Draw a **No Smoking** sign on the board. Say, *Look at the sign.* Have learners repeat. Pantomime smoking and ask learners what the sign says (*No smoking*).

PRESENTATION

1. Focus attention on the illustration. Help learners say as much as they can about it. You may want to cue them by indicating the

items for learners to say, or by saying names of items and having learners indicate them. Restate their ideas in acceptable English and write them on the board or overhead projector.

Present the dialog. See "Presenting Dialogs" on page viii.

2. Help learners read the directions. Demonstrate by reading the words aloud. Then have learners complete the activity in pairs. Ask volunteers to read the words aloud.

3. Help learners read the directions. Then present the listening activity. See "Presenting Listening Activities" on page ix. Check learners' work. Ask volunteers to read their answers aloud.

4. Help learners read the directions. Demonstrate by completing the first item on the board or overhead projector. Have learners complete the exercise independently. Check learners' work.

5. Help learners read the directions. Demonstrate by completing the first item on the board or overhead projector. Then ask learners to complete the exercise independently. Check learners' work. Ask volunteers to read their answers aloud.

FOLLOW-UP

Reading Signs: Bring in examples of cleaning supplies and other materials used in learners' workplaces. Have learners look for the words **Danger, Poison,** and **No Smoking.** Point

4. Circle.

Circle DANGER, NO SMOKING, **and** POISON.
Say the words.

5. Circle.

Are they following the signs? Circle yes **or** no.

a. yes (no)

b. yes (no)

c. yes (no)

d. (yes) no

Unit 8

`91`

out other words and symbols used to indicate dangerous materials, such as **Hazardous, Flammable,** and **Caution.** Ask questions about the materials, such as, *Can I smoke near this material? Can I touch this? Is it OK to drink this?*

♦ As a group, create a list of the warning words. Distribute copies of the list for learners to take with them and have learners check which words they see in their workplaces and homes. Ask learners to share their lists with the class. Discuss why it is important to recognize the signs and how to store hazardous materials safely.

★   ★   ★   ★   ★

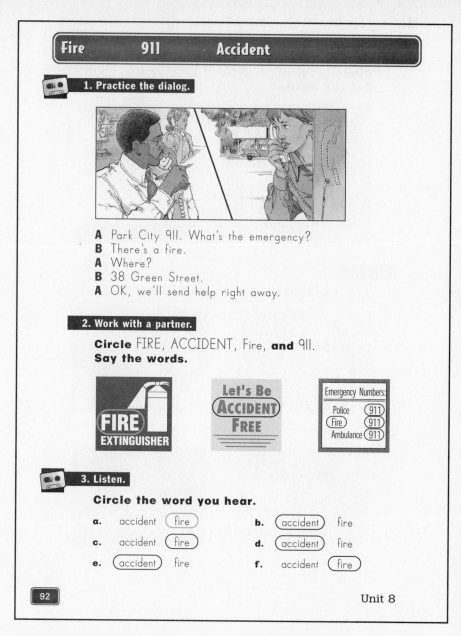

Fire   911   Accident

1. Practice the dialog.

A Park City 911. What's the emergency?
B There's a fire.
A Where?
B 38 Green Street.
A OK, we'll send help right away.

2. Work with a partner.

Circle FIRE, ACCIDENT, Fire, **and** 911.
Say the words.

FIRE EXTINGUISHER

Let's Be ACCIDENT FREE

Emergency Numbers:
Police (911)
Fire (911)
Ambulance (911)

3. Listen.

Circle the word you hear.

a. accident (fire)   b. (accident) fire
c. accident (fire)   d. (accident) fire
e. (accident) fire   f. accident (fire)

92   Unit 8

Culture Note

*You might want to point out that in case of fire, everyone should leave the building immediately. No one should try to call 911 from **inside** a burning building. Also, people should use the stairs rather than the elevator during a fire unless instructed otherwise by firefighters.*

PREPARATION

Preteach the new language in the lesson. Follow these suggestions.

• Use picture cards and word cards to preteach the words **fire, 911,** and **accident.** See "Presenting Recognition Words" on page viii.

• To preteach the word **emergency,** show the picture cards for **fire** and **accident.** Say, *These are emergencies.*

• Write an address on the board or overhead projector. Draw a building with smoke and/or fire coming from it. Look alarmed and say, *There's a fire.* Have learners repeat. Then ask, *Where?* Have learners repeat. Say the address and have learners repeat.

• Preteach the dialog. To teach *We'll send help right away,* write the address

38 Green Street on the board above the chalk rail. Put the picture of the fire truck on the chalk rail at the other end of the board and move the picture along the rail to the address.

• Use Blackline Master 10: Telephone to have learners practice dialing 911.

PRESENTATION

 1. Focus attention on the illustration. Have learners say as much as they can about it. You may want to cue them by indicating the items and having learners say the names, or by saying names of items and having learners indicate them. Restate their ideas in acceptable English and write them on the board or overhead projector.

Present the dialog. See "Presenting Dialogs" on page viii.

2. Help learners read the directions. Demonstrate by completing the first item on the board or overhead projector. Then have learners complete the activity. Check learners' work. Go over the answers on the board or overhead projector. Have volunteers read the words aloud.

 3. Help learners read the directions. Then present the listening activity. See "Presenting Listening Activities" on page ix. Check learners' work. Ask volunteers to read their answers aloud.

4. Help learners read the directions. Model writing the words on the board or overhead projector and saying the words aloud. Have learners complete the exercise. Check learners' work. For

4. Write.

Write the words and numbers.
Say the words and numbers.

fire	_____	_____
fire	_____	_____
accident	_____	_____
911	_____	_____

5. Work with a partner.

Where's the fire? Where's the accident?
Write the addresses.

a. _____73 Bank Street_____   b. _____25 North Street_____

6. Work with a partner.

Practice calling 911. Use the places in 5.

A Hope Town 911. What's the emergency?

B There's a _____fire_____.

A Where?

B _____73 Bank Street._____

A OK, we'll send help right away.

Unit 8   93

---

extra reinforcement, use Blackline Master 5: Lined Paper.

5. Help learners read the directions. Demonstrate by completing the first item on the board or overhead projector. Then ask learners to work with a partner to complete the activity. Check learners' work. Ask volunteers to read the addresses aloud.

6. Help learners read the directions. Demonstrate by saying the dialog with a volunteer. Have learners say the dialog in pairs. Have learners change partners and repeat several times. Ask several pairs to say their conversations for the class.

FOLLOW-UP

Fire Drill: Take the class on a trip through the building. Help learners recognize emergency equipment, alarms, and emergency exits. Have learners point out words that they recognize. Help learners determine how to leave the building quickly and safely.

♦ Ask learners to plan and mark the best route out of the building on the floor plans made in Unit 2. Encourage learners to talk about how they would exit from their workplaces in case of fire. If possible, have a fire drill for your class, without sounding the alarm, so learners know what to do.

WORKFORCE SKILLS (pages 94-95)

State symptoms and injuries

Call 911

Follow safety instructions

★　　★　　★　　★　　★

Language Note

In English there are many places where people can go for health care. People go to the doctor's office, to the hospital, to the clinic, to the health center, or to the emergency room for health care. Have learners discuss the kinds of health care providers they go to.

Hospital　　　Emergency Room

 1. Practice the dialog.

A What's the matter?
B My leg is hurt.
A You need to go to the emergency room.

 2. Work with a partner.

Circle Hospital **and** Emergency Room.
Say the words.

`94`

Unit 8

PREPARATION

Preteach the new language in the lesson. Follow these suggestions.

● Use word cards and picture cards to introduce the words **hospital** and **emergency room.** See "Presenting Recognition Words" on page viii.

● Preteach the dialog. Ask a volunteer to pantomime having an injured leg. Ask, *What's the matter?* Prompt the volunteer to respond, *My leg is hurt.* Then say, *You need to go to the emergency room.* Have learners repeat. Put the picture card and the word card for **emergency room** on a desk or on the board. Then help the volunteer to where the card is, as if you are "going" to the emergency room.

PRESENTATION

1. Focus attention on the illustration. Have learners say as much as they can about it. You may want to cue them by indicating the items and having learners say the names, or by saying names of items and having learners indicate them. Restate their ideas in acceptable English and write them on the board or overhead projector.

Present the dialog. See "Presenting Dialogs" on page viii.

2. Help learners read the directions. Demonstrate by completing the first item on the board or overhead projector. Then have learners complete the exercise in pairs. Check learners' work. Ask volunteers to say the words aloud.

3. Help learners read the directions. Then present the listening activity. See "Presenting Listening Activities" on page ix. Check learners' work. Ask volunteers to read their answers aloud.

4. Help learners read the directions. Demonstrate by completing the first item on the board or overhead projector. Then have learners complete the exercise. Check learners' work. For extra reinforcement, use Blackline Master 5: Lined Paper.

5. Help learners read the directions. Demonstrate by completing the first item on the board or overhead projector. Have learners complete the exercise in pairs. Check learners' work. Then demonstrate saying the dialog with a volunteer. Have learners say the

3. Listen.

What do the people do? Circle.

a. (Go to the hospital.) Call 911.

b. Go to the hospital. (Call 911.)

c. Go to the hospital. (Call 911.)

d. (Go to the hospital.) Call 911.

4. Write.

hospital _____ _____

emergency room _____ _____

5. Work with a partner.

Complete the dialog. Practice the dialog.

| cut | emergency | hand | Hospital |

A What's the matter?

B My ___hand___ is ___cut___ .

A You need to go to the ___emergency___ room at

City ___Hospital___ .

Unit 8   95

---

dialog in pairs. Have learners change partners and repeat. Ask several pairs to say their conversations for the class.

FOLLOW-UP

First-Aid Kit: Bring a first-aid kit to class. Help learners identify the contents and the problem each item is used to treat.

♦ Help learners prepare a list of information that 911 or emergency room workers might ask about an injured person. Have learners role-play calling 911 about an injured coworker or friend.

Look.

What's missing from the signs? Write the words.

| Danger | Fire | No Smoking | Poison |

a. _____Danger_____

b. _____No Smoking_____

c. _____Poison_____

d. _____Fire_____ Extinguisher

96

Unit 8

PREPARATION

Review the new language using the following suggestions.

● Write the words **Danger, Fire, No Smoking,** and **Poison** on the board or overhead projector. Ask volunteers to read the words aloud and find a matching illustration in the book for each one.

PRESENTATION

Help learners read the directions. Focus attention on the illustrations. Ask learners to say as much as they can about them. Restate learners' ideas in acceptable English and write them on the board or overhead projector. Demonstrate by completing the first item on the board or overhead projector. Have learners complete the exercise individually. Check learners' work. Ask a different learner to say each answer aloud.

FOLLOW-UP

Warning Signs: Help learners create a list of warning signs they have seen in the building, at work, or in the community. If possible, list the signs and the places where they are found. Explain the meanings as needed.

♦ Using the information from the previous activity, learners can make posters showing warning signs. Individuals can present their posters to the class and tell where the signs would be seen.

Performance Check

1. Write the word.

| arm | foot | hand | leg |

a. leg b. hand c. foot d. arm

2. Write.

Complete the sentences.

| fire | hurt |

a. Her back is ___hurt___. b. There's a ___fire___.

3. Circle.

Look at the pictures. Circle the words.

a. Danger (No Smoking) b. (Poison) Accident

Unit 8   97

ASAP PROJECT

Help learners prepare a First-Aid Booklet. As a group, brainstorm injuries and illnesses and how to deal with them: by going to the emergency room, visiting a clinic or doctor's office, or using simple first aid. Then ask learners to each choose a different situation to illustrate for the booklet. They may work in pairs or groups if necessary. Encourage them to label the injury or illness, tell who or where to go for help, and any other information they would like to write about it.

Compile the pages to form a booklet. If possible, duplicate the booklet so each learner has a copy.

Learners should use the booklet to check what to do in different emergency situations.

PREPARATION

Briefly review the new language before learners open their books. Follow these suggestions.

● Write the recognition words for parts of the body and injuries on the board or overhead projector and display picture cards for the words. Have volunteers match the words with the appropriate pictures and say the words.

● Write the words **Accident, Fire, Danger, No Smoking,** and **Poison** on the board or overhead projector. Ask volunteers to read the words aloud and find a matching illustration in the book for each one.

Provide specific help as needed until you are sure learners feel confident that they know all the new words.

PRESENTATION

Use any of the procedures in "Evaluation," page ix, with this page. Record individuals' results on the Unit 8 Individual Competency Chart. Record the class's results on the Class Cumulative Competency Chart.

INFORMAL WORKPLACE-SPECIFIC ASSESSMENT

Ask learners to name or identify a safety sign related to their workplace or job interests. Have the learner explain what the sign means.

Unit 9 Overview

—SCANS Competencies—

★ Recognize teamwork skills

★ Participate as a member of a team

★ Interpret/communicate information

★ Work with people from culturally diverse backgrounds

★ Allocate time

★ Monitor and correct performance

Unit 9 Workforce Skills

● Introduce oneself

● Greet coworkers

● Get along with coworkers

● Accept feedback and correct errors

● Understand company rules

Materials

● Picture and word cards for **coworkers, supervisor, break,** and **lunch.** Word cards for **Nice to meet you, Where are you from?, Good work,** and **I'm sorry.**

● Pictures of grass, people working in teams, people doing good work and poor work, and workers who need to wear safety glasses and gloves

● Realia: magazines, a world map, a clock with moveable hands, dishes, safety glasses, and gloves

● Blackline Master 11: Clock

★   ★   ★   ★   ★

UNIT **9** **Working with People**

Look at the pictures.

What are the people doing?

Do you work with other people?

Who do you work with?

98

Unit 9

WORKFORCE SKILLS (page 98)

Recognize teamwork skills

Get along with coworkers

★   ★   ★   ★   ★

Teaching Note

Use Blackline Masters 6 and 7: Common Directions to clarify the directions in this unit. Use page 98 to warm up learners, to draw on prior knowledge, and to spark interest.

PRESENTATION

Focus attention on the illustrations. Have learners say as much as they can about them. Learners may be able to name a few items in the pictures, but you may have to prompt them by naming items and having learners repeat. You also might read the unit title and questions aloud and have learners answer the questions. Model any words learners do not know.

FOLLOW-UP

Pictures of Workers: Provide pairs of learners with magazines. Ask learners to cut out pictures of people working together. Have each pair of learners show their pictures to the class and say if the people are a good team. Help learners say where the people work and what they do. Provide feedback as necessary.

♦ Divide the class into several teams. Have learners choose team reporters. Have teams share their pictures from the first part of the activity and sort them into categories, such as working with a partner or working with a team. Circulate and help learners name the categories they decide upon. Then let the team reporters share the categories and pictures with the class.

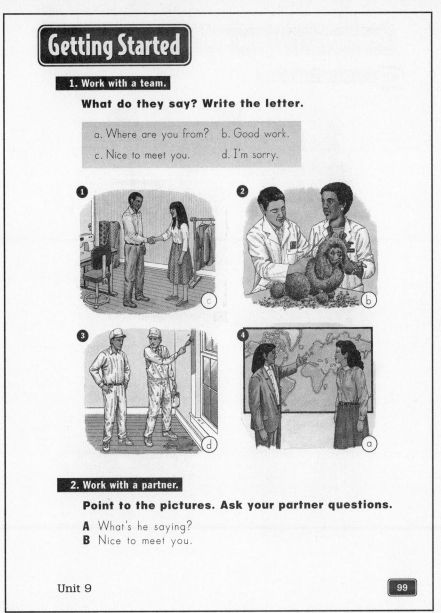

Getting Started

1. Work with a team.

What do they say? Write the letter.

a. Where are you from?　b. Good work.

c. Nice to meet you.　　d. I'm sorry.

2. Work with a partner.

Point to the pictures. Ask your partner questions.

A What's he saying?
B Nice to meet you.

Unit 9

99

Teaching Note

Use this page to introduce the new language in the unit. Whenever possible, encourage peer teaching. Supply any language the learners need.

PREPARATION

Focus attention on the illustrations. Have learners say as much as they can about them. Learners may be able to name a few items in the pictures, but you may have to prompt them by naming items and having learners repeat.

Preteach the new language in the lesson. Follow these suggestions.

● Use word cards, the map, and pantomime to introduce or review the words and expressions **Nice to meet you, Where are you from? I'm sorry,** and **Good work.**

PRESENTATION

1. Help learners read the directions. Demonstrate by completing the first item on the board or overhead projector. Have learners complete the exercise in teams. Encourage learners to work together. Go over the answers with the class.

2. Help learners read the directions. Model the dialog as learners listen. Say the dialog again and have learners repeat. Ask learners to practice the dialog with a partner. Then model substituting the next item on the page in the dialog, and ask learners to continue similarly with the remaining items.

FOLLOW-UP

What Am I Saying? Have learners act out a scenario portraying one of the expressions on the page. Have the rest of the class figure out which expression they are portraying.

◆ Help learners brainstorm other expressions related to meeting people and receiving feedback that they might hear at work. Write the expressions on the board and help learners say them.

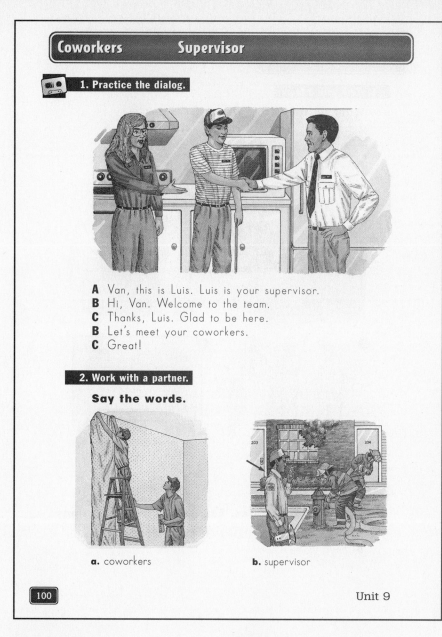

Coworkers　　　Supervisor

1. Practice the dialog.

A Van, this is Luis. Luis is your supervisor.
B Hi, Van. Welcome to the team.
C Thanks, Luis. Glad to be here.
B Let's meet your coworkers.
C Great!

2. Work with a partner.

Say the words.

a. coworkers

b. supervisor

100

Unit 9

Language Note

Learners may hear supervisors called by different names. You might present a few common alternatives: **boss, team leader, captain, manager, foreman, superintendent,** *etc.*

PREPARATION

Preteach the new language in the lesson. Follow these suggestions.

● Use word cards and picture cards to preteach the recognition words **coworkers** and **supervisor.** See "Presenting Recognition Words" on page viii.

● Preteach the dialog. Ask a volunteer to leave the room and re-enter. Say, *Hi, (name). Welcome to the class.* Motion towards the other learners in the class and say, *Let's meet your classmates.* Have learners repeat. Then introduce the volunteer to several classmates.

PRESENTATION

 1. Focus attention on the illustration. Help learners speculate about the place and who the people are. Have them say as much as they can about the illustration. You may want to indicate items in the illustration for learners to say, or say names of items and have learners indicate them. Restate learners' ideas in acceptable English and write them on the board or overhead projector.

Present the dialog. See "Presenting Dialogs" on page viii.

2. Help learners read the directions. Demonstrate by indicating the first picture and saying the word **coworkers.** Then have learners complete the exercise in pairs. Have volunteers say the words aloud to the class.

3. Help learners read the directions. Then present the listening activity. See "Presenting Listening Activities" on page ix. Check learners' work. Ask volunteers to read their answers aloud.

4. Help learners read the directions. Demonstrate by completing the first item on the board or overhead projector. Have learners complete the exercise independently. Then check learners' work.

5. Help learners read the directions. Demonstrate by completing the first item on the board or overhead projector. Have learners complete the exercise. Check learners' work.

 6. Help learners read the directions. Demonstrate by completing the information

3. Listen.

Circle the word you hear.

a. coworkers (supervisor)   b. (coworkers) supervisor

c. (coworkers) supervisor   d. coworkers (supervisor)

4. Look.

Circle the supervisors.

5. Write.

Write the words. Say the words.

coworkers	_____	_____	_____
coworkers	_____	_____	_____
supervisor	_____	_____	_____
supervisor	_____	_____	_____

6. Write.

Write the names of people from your workplace or class.

Coworkers: _____

Supervisor: _____

Unit 9

101

about yourself on the board or overhead projector. Then have learners complete the exercise independently. Check learners' work. Ask volunteers to read the names of their coworkers and supervisors aloud.

FOLLOW-UP

Who Are They? Bring in pictures of work teams and have learners work in groups to identify who the coworkers are and who the supervisors are. Have groups present their pictures and ideas to the class.

♦ Using the dialog on page 100 as a model, have groups write dialogs based on their pictures. Then have groups present their dialogs to the class.

Greet coworkers

Introduce yourself

★　　★　　★　　★　　★

Culture Note

Tell learners that English speakers usually make eye contact when greeting others. Show them how to take your hand firmly when shaking it. Then have learners shake hands with each other.

Introductions

 1. Practice the dialog.

A Hi, I'm Lin.
B Nice to meet you, Lin. I'm Ted.
A Nice to meet you, Ted.
B Where are you from, Lin?
A I'm from Korea. Where are you from?
B I'm from Los Angeles.

2. Match.

**What do they say? Write the letter.
Say the words.**

a. Where are you from?
b. Nice to meet you.

102   Unit 9

PREPARATION

Preteach the new language in the lesson. Follow these suggestions.

● Use word cards and pantomime to preteach the introduction words **Nice to meet you** and **Where are you from?** See "Presenting Recognition Words" on page viii.

● To show how English speakers greet and introduce themselves, ask a volunteer to shake hands with you. Say, *Hi, I'm (your name).* Have the learner repeat with his/her name. Then say, *Nice to meet you.* Have the learner repeat. Then have the class repeat.

● Tell learners your name and home country. Say, *I'm (name) and I'm from (country).* Then put a marker on the map to represent your home country.

Have learners give the same information about themselves. Help them put markers on the map to indicate their home countries. Model asking and answering questions about native countries. Ask, *Where are you from?* Have learners repeat. Say, *I'm from (country).* Ask volunteers to tell where they are from in response to the question.

PRESENTATION

 1. Focus attention on the illustration. Have learners say as much as they can about it. You may want to cue them by indicating the items and having learners say the names, or by saying names of items and having learners indicate them. Restate learners' ideas in acceptable English and write them on the board or overhead projector.

Present the dialogs. See "Presenting Dialogs" on page viii.

2. Help learners read the directions and the answer choices. Then have learners complete the exercise independently. Check the exercise on the board or overhead projector. Ask volunteers to read the answers aloud.

 3. Help learners read the directions. Then present the listening activity. See "Presenting Listening Activities" on page ix. Check learners' work. Ask volunteers to read their answers aloud.

4. Help learners read the directions. Demonstrate by completing the first item on the board or overhead projector. Then have learners complete the exercise independently. Ask volunteers to read the words aloud.

---

3. Listen.

Do you hear Nice to meet you? **Circle** yes **or** no.

a. (yes)   no   **b.** (yes)   no

c. (yes)   no   **d.** yes   (no)

4. Write.

Write the words. Say the words.

_____Nice to meet you._____   _____Where are you from?_____

_____   _____

_____   _____

_____   _____

5. Write.

Complete the dialog.

from	Hi	meet	Nice	Where

A _____Hi_____ , I'm Anton.

B Nice to _____meet_____ you, Anton. I'm Mei.

A _____Nice_____ to meet you, Mei.

B Where are you _____from_____ , Anton?

A I'm from Russia. _____Where_____ are you from?

B I'm from China.

6. Work with a partner.

Practice the dialog in 5. Use your own names and countries.

Teaching Note

Encourage learners to repeat the name of the person they are talking to during greetings and introductions. Repetition will help them remember the person's name and show they take an interest in that person.

Unit 9   103

---

5. Help learners read the directions. Ask volunteers to read the words in the box aloud. Demonstrate by completing the first item on the board or overhead projector. Then ask learners to complete the exercise independently. Check learners' work. Ask volunteers to read the answers aloud.

6. Help learners read the directions. Demonstrate by saying the dialog with a volunteer. Then have learners say the dialog in pairs. Have learners change partners and repeat several times. Ask several pairs to say their conversations for the class.

FOLLOW-UP

My Country: Have learners bring in photographs taken in their countries of origin, items of clothing typical of their countries, or objects from their countries. Have each learner in turn name his or her country, indicate it on the world map, and show what he or she brought in.

♦ Arrange learners in pairs to tell each other their countries of origin and show each other the items they've brought in. Then have pairs join to form groups of four. Within the groups, have each learner tell the others what country his or her partner is from and what item his or her partner brought in.

WORKFORCE SKILLS (pages 104–105)

Understand company rules

Get along with coworkers

★　　　★　　　★　　　★　　　★

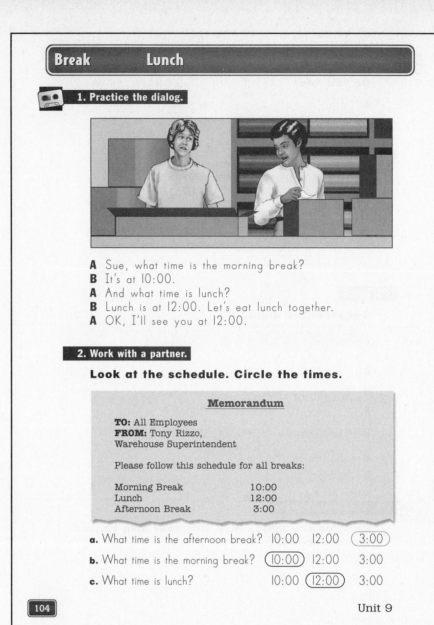

Break　　　　Lunch

 1. Practice the dialog.

A Sue, what time is the morning break?
B It's at 10:00.
A And what time is lunch?
B Lunch is at 12:00. Let's eat lunch together.
A OK, I'll see you at 12:00.

2. Work with a partner.

Look at the schedule. Circle the times.

> **Memorandum**
>
> **TO:** All Employees
> **FROM:** Tony Rizzo,
> Warehouse Superintendent
>
> Please follow this schedule for all breaks:
>
> Morning Break　　　　10:00
> Lunch　　　　　　　　12:00
> Afternoon Break　　　3:00

a. What time is the afternoon break?　10:00　12:00　(3:00)

b. What time is the morning break?　(10:00)　12:00　3:00

c. What time is lunch?　10:00　(12:00)　3:00

104　　　　　　　　　　　　　　　　　　　Unit 9

Teaching Note

*Depending on the shifts that learners work, you may want to introduce other break-related words, such as **dinner**, as needed.*

PREPARATION

Preteach the new language in the lesson. Follow these suggestions.

● Review time by using Blackline Master 11: Clock or an analog clock with moveable hands. Follow the suggestions on page 46. Show various times on the clock and have learners say the times. Ask, *What time do you start work? What time do you go home?* Help learners say the times and set the clock to show those times.

● Use picture cards, word cards, and pantomime to preteach the words **break** and **lunch.** See "Presenting Recognition Words" on page viii.

● Preteach the dialog. Show the picture card for **break** and model the question, *What time is the morning break?* Have

learners repeat. Ask a volunteer to show on the clock and write on the board the time he or she has his/her morning break. Model the response, *It's at (time).* Repeat the same procedure with the picture card for **lunch** to preteach the question and answer about lunch time. Then gesture to a learner and yourself and say, *Let's each lunch together.* Have learners repeat. Model the response, *OK, I'll see you at 12:00.* Ask learners to repeat.

PRESENTATION

1. Focus attention on the illustration. Have learners say as much as they can about it. You may want to cue them by indicating the items and having learners say the names, or by saying names of items and having

learners indicate them. Restate learners' ideas in acceptable English and write them on the board or overhead projector.

Present the dialog. See "Presenting Dialogs" on page viii.

2. Read the questions aloud. Ask volunteers to answer about their workplace or school. Then help learners read the directions and the memorandum. Demonstrate by completing the first item on the board or overhead projector. Then have learners answer the questions. Check learners' work. Ask volunteers to say their answers aloud and indicate the appropriate time on the clock.

3. Listen.

Circle the words you hear.

a. lunch (afternoon break)   b. (morning break) lunch

c. lunch (afternoon break)   d. morning break (lunch)

4. Write.

Write the words. Say the words.

break _____ _____ _____

lunch _____ _____ _____

5. Write.

Complete the schedule.
Write about your workplace or school.

SCHEDULE

MORNING BREAK _____

LUNCH _____

AFTERNOON BREAK _____

6. Work with a partner.

Ask your partner about his or her schedule.
Write his or her answers. Then practice the dialog.

A What time is your morning break?

B It's at _____ .

A And what time is lunch?

B Lunch is at _____ .

Unit 9   105

---

3. Help learners read the directions. Then present the listening activity. See "Presenting Listening Activities" on page ix. Check learners' work. Ask volunteers to read their answers aloud.

4. Help learners read the directions. Demonstrate by completing the first item on the board or overhead projector. Have learners complete the exercise independently. Ask volunteers to read the words aloud and match them to the picture cards.

5. Help learners read the directions. Demonstrate on the board or overhead projector using information about your own work schedule. Have learners complete the activity independently. Check learners' work.

6. Help learners read the directions. Demonstrate saying the dialog with a volunteer. Write his or her answers on the board. Then have learners complete the activity. Have learners change partners and repeat the activity several times. Ask several pairs to say their dialogs for the class.

FOLLOW-UP

Illustrated Schedule: Provide each learner with a 3-column chart. Instruct each learner to create a schedule for his/her work or school. In the first column, have them write the times they start work/school, take a break, have lunch (or another meal/snack), and go home. In the second column, have learners write a word or phrase to describe the activity at that time. In the third column, learners can draw a picture for the activities. Invite volunteers to show and explain their schedules to the class.

♦ Display learners' schedules. As a group, compare similarities and differences they see in the schedules. Encourage learners to suggest reasons for the similarities and differences.

WORKFORCE SKILLS (pages 106–107)

Accept feedback and correct errors

★   ★   ★   ★   ★

SCANS Note

*You might point out that in some workplaces, supervisors are addressed by the titles **Mr., Ms., Miss,** or **Mrs.** and last name, while in other workplaces, supervisors are addressed by their first names.*

Good work

 1. Practice the dialogs.

A These dishes look great. Good work!
B Thank you, Ms. Green.

A That grass doesn't look very good. Please cut it again.
B Oh, I'm sorry. I'll cut it again now.

2. Work with a partner.

Do they say Good work? **Circle** yes **or** no.

a. (yes) no   **b.** yes (no)   **c.** (yes) no

106   Unit 9

PREPARATION

Preteach the new language in the lesson. Follow these suggestions.

● Use pictures or the illustrations on the page and pantomime to show examples of good and poor work. Show the word card **Good work** and model the expression. Have learners repeat. As you show pictures or act out examples of good work, have learners say, *Good work.* See "Presenting Recognition Words" on page viii.

● Preteach the dialogs. Hold up some clean dishes and say, *These dishes look great. Good work!* Have learners repeat. Model the response *Thank you* and have learners repeat. Then have learners look at the picture card of grass. Model the word and have learners repeat. Then draw some long grass on the board with the green chalk. Say, *That grass doesn't look very good. Please cut it again.* Ask learners to repeat. Then model the response, *I'm sorry. I'll cut it again now.* Pantomime mowing the lawn. Have learners repeat.

PRESENTATION

 1. Focus attention on the illustrations. Have learners say as much as they can about them. You may want to cue them by indicating the items for learners to name, or by saying names of items and having learners indicate them. Restate their ideas in acceptable English and write them on the board or overhead projector.

Present the dialogs. See "Presenting Dialogs" on page viii.

2. Help learners read the directions. Demonstrate by circling the answer to the first item on the board or overhead projector. Then have them complete the activity independently. Check learners' work. Ask volunteers to say the answers aloud.

 3. Help learners read the directions. Then present the listening activity. See "Presenting Listening Activities" on page ix. Check learners' work. Ask volunteers to read their answers aloud.

4. Help learners read the directions. Demonstrate by completing the first item on the board or overhead projector. Then have learners complete the exercise independently. Ask volunteers to read the words aloud.

                                           English ASAP

3. Listen.

Do you hear Good work? **Circle** yes **or** no.

a. (yes)   no   b. yes   (no)

c. (yes)   no   d. (yes)   no

4. Write.

Write the words. Say the words.

good work _____ _____

good work _____ _____

good work _____ _____

5. Write.

What do they say? Write I'm sorry **or** Thank you.

A These copies look great. Good work!

B _Thank you_, Mr. Hill.

A These towels don't look very good. Please wash them again.

B _I'm sorry_. I'll wash them again now.

6. Work with a partner.

Practice the dialogs in 5.

Unit 9

107

---

5. Help learners read the directions. Demonstrate by completing the first item on the board or overhead projector. Have learners complete the activity independently. Check learners' work. Then ask volunteers to read the answers aloud.

6. Help learners read the directions. Demonstrate with a volunteer. Then have pairs of learners complete the activity. Have learners change partners and repeat the activity several times. Ask several pairs to say their conversations for the class.

FOLLOW-UP

You're the Supervisor: On index cards, write some simple commands learners know, such as, **Put the book on the top shelf.** Demonstrate taking a card, asking

someone to do the task, and then telling the person if he/she did a good job or needs to do something differently. If the person performs the job correctly, say, *Good work.* If the job is not completely correct, ask the person to correct it. Invite volunteers to take a card and give instructions for other volunteers.

♦ Divide learners into groups. Each group should have its own set of tasks on cards. Learners can take turns being the supervisor and giving commands and feedback about the others' work.

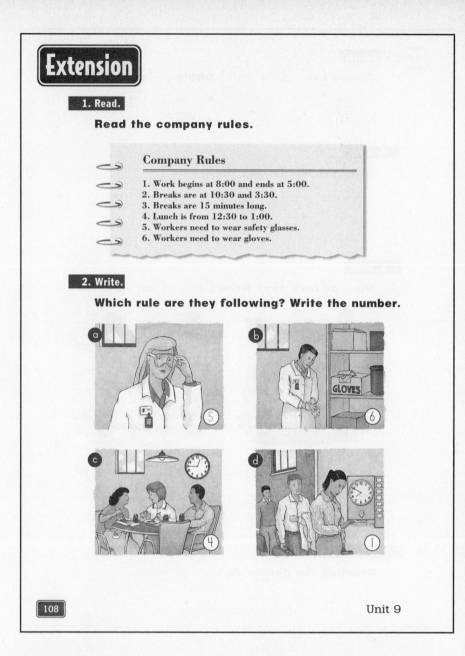

Extension

1. Read.

Read the company rules.

Company Rules

1. Work begins at 8:00 and ends at 5:00.
2. Breaks are at 10:30 and 3:30.
3. Breaks are 15 minutes long.
4. Lunch is from 12:30 to 1:00.
5. Workers need to wear safety glasses.
6. Workers need to wear gloves.

2. Write.

Which rule are they following? Write the number.

a. 5

b. 6

c. 4

d. 1

Unit 9

PREPARATION

Preteach or review the new language using the following suggestions.

● If necessary, review time by following the suggestions on page 104.

● On the board or overhead projector, write the words **break** and **lunch.** Ask volunteers to read the words aloud and find the matching picture cards for the words.

● Ask a volunteer when his/her break time is at work (or at school). Write **(Name)'s break begins at (time)** on the board. Ask when the break ends. Write **(Name)'s break ends at (time)** on the board. You may want to use an analog clock or Blackline Master 11: Clock to clarify how many minutes are in the break. Write on the board the length of

the break: **(Name)'s break is (number) minutes long.**

● Bring in pictures of safety glasses and gloves or use realia. Write the words **gloves** and **safety glasses** on the board or overhead projector. Ask volunteers to read the words aloud. As they read the words, hold up the picture card or item.

PRESENTATION

1. Help learners read the directions. Focus attention on the list of company rules and discuss it with the class. Help learners read the rules. Ask a few questions to make sure learners understand, such as, *What time is lunch? Is the morning break at 8:00?*

2. Help learners read the directions. Demonstrate by writing the answer to the first item on the board or overhead

projector. Then have learners complete the exercise independently. Check learners' work.

FOLLOW-UP

Matching Safety Equipment and Jobs: Provide learners with picture cards for jobs. Have learners select jobs where workers need to wear gloves and safety glasses.

♦ As a class, make a list of jobs (using words or pictures) that require safety equipment. Supply any language needed. Encourage learners to think about other jobs they know from their own experiences that require safety equipment. Add these jobs to the list.

Performance Check

1. Write

Write coworkers **or** supervisor.

a. _coworkers_ **b.** _supervisor_ **c.** _coworkers_

2. Write.

Complete the dialog.

| Hi | meet | Nice |

A _____Hi_____ , I'm Elena.

B Nice to _____meet_____ you, Elena. I'm Richard.

A _____Nice_____ to meet you, too, Richard.

3. Write.

Write Thank you **or** I'm sorry.

A These towels look great. Good work! **A** These copies don't look very good. Please copy the forms again.

B _Thank you_ , Mrs. Li. **B** _I'm sorry_ , Ms. West. I'll copy them again now.

Unit 9

109

ASAP
PROJECT

Bring in examples of workplace rules or have learners refer to the list on page 108. Help learners create their own set of rules for the classroom, their own workplace, or a fictitious workplace. Brainstorm a list of ideas. Have learners or groups of learners each choose one of the ideas and prepare a written rule. Each learner or group should choose a different idea. Encourage learners to read and comment on each other's work and make suggestions. After learners make final copies of their rules, they can cut out magazine pictures or make drawings to illustrate their rules. Compile the rules in a booklet. If possible, make copies and distribute them to the class.

PREPARATION

Briefly review the new language before learners open their books. Follow these suggestions.

● Review **coworkers** and **supervisor** using word cards and picture cards. Have learners say the words.

● Review greetings and introductions using word cards and by having learners greet each other. Have learners say the expressions.

● Review giving feedback on work. Have learners respond to compliments and corrections with *Thank you* or *I'm sorry.*

Provide specific help as needed until you are sure learners feel confident that they know all the new words and language.

PRESENTATION

Use any of the procedures in "Evaluation," page ix, with this page. Record individuals' results on the Unit 9 Individual Competency Chart. Record the class's results on the Class Cumulative Competency Chart.

INFORMAL WORKPLACE-SPECIFIC ASSESSMENT

Ask learners to name their coworkers and supervisors. Ask them to name a rule or piece of safety equipment from their workplaces.

Unit 10 Overview

—SCANS Competencies—

★ Acquire and evaluate information
★ Interpret and communicate information
★ Allocate time
★ Negotiate

Unit 10 Workforce Skills

• Identify kinds of jobs
• Give one's work experience
• Read help-wanted ads and signs
• Complete a simple job application

Materials

• Picture and word cards for **days** and **nights**
• Word cards for **application, experience, weekends, help wanted, full time,** and **part time**
• Picture and word cards for jobs and workplaces in the unit (painter, custodian, cook, clerk, mechanic, housekeeper, kitchen, office, auto repair shop, and hotel)
• Realia: a calendar, the help-wanted section of a newspaper, job applications, magazines
• Blackline Master 9: Job Application

★　　★　　★　　★　　★

UNIT 10 **Career Development**

Look at the pictures.

Name the jobs.

What are some other workplaces?

Where do you work?

110

Unit 10

WORKFORCE SKILLS (page 110)

Identify kinds of jobs

★　　★　　★　　★　　★

Teaching Note

Use Blackline Masters 6 and 7: Common Directions to clarify the directions in this unit. Use page 110 to warm up learners, to draw on prior knowledge, and to spark interest.

PREPARATION

Begin the class by showing pictures of jobs. Help learners identify the jobs and possible workplaces. Ask learners about jobs they have now or had in the past.

PRESENTATION

Focus attention on the illustrations. Have learners say as much as they can about them. Learners may be able to name a few people, places, or items in the pictures, but you will probably have to prompt them by naming items and having learners repeat. You also might read the unit title and questions aloud and have learners answer the questions. Model any words learners do not know.

Ask learners if they have seen or know people with these jobs. If so, encourage them to share information they know about these jobs and any others that they are familiar with.

FOLLOW-UP

Jobs and Workplaces: Help learners brainstorm a list of workplaces. Then help learners develop a list of jobs that might be available at each workplace. Encourage learners to pantomime the jobs if they don't know the words for them. Supply any vocabulary needed. Write the words on the board or overhead projector and read them aloud.

♦ Ask learners to think about the lists of jobs and identify which ones might be available in your community. If learners work or have applied for jobs, encourage them to share their experiences with the class.

English ASAP

Getting Started

1. Work with a team.

Match.

2. Work with a partner.

Which job can you do? Circle the picture.
Show your partner.

Unit 10

111

Teaching Note

Use this page to introduce the new language in the unit. Whenever possible, encourage peer teaching. Supply any language the learners need.

PREPARATION

Focus attention on the illustrations. Have learners say as much as they can about them. You may have to prompt learners by naming people, places, and items in the pictures and having learners repeat.

PRESENTATION

1. Help learners read the directions. Demonstrate by completing the first item on the board or overhead projector. Have learners complete the exercise in teams. Encourage learners to work together. Go over the answers with the class.

 2. Help learners read the directions. Demonstrate by circling on the board or overhead projector a job that you can do.

Have learners circle the job or jobs that they can do.

Ask learners to show their choices to a partner. Encourage learners to identify their partners' choices. Have learners change partners and repeat the activity. Ask volunteers to tell the class about their answers.

FOLLOW-UP

Job Collage: Arrange learners in groups. Give each group a large sheet of paper with a picture of a workplace in the center. Have learners look through magazines for pictures of jobs that might be found at the workplace. Learners should create a collage by pasting or gluing the pictures around the workplace. Have groups show their collages to the class.

♦ Help learners label the jobs and workplaces. Ask volunteers to show their groups' collages and to identify the jobs and workplaces.

WORKFORCE SKILLS (pages 112–113)

Identify kinds of jobs

Give one's work experience

★   ★   ★   ★   ★

Teaching Note

In this lesson, you might also present the names of jobs available to learners in your community or jobs that learners actually have.

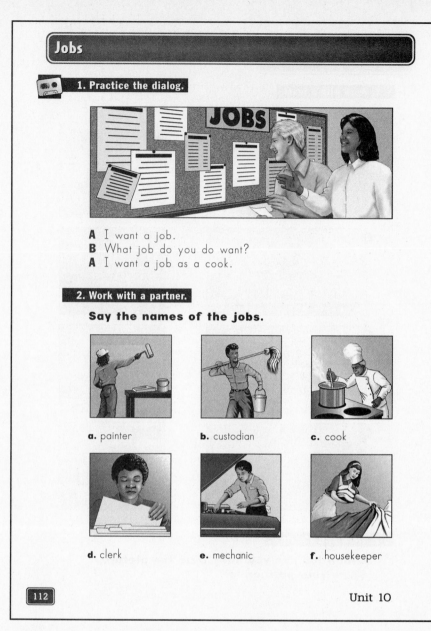

Jobs

1. Practice the dialog.

A I want a job.
B What job do you do want?
A I want a job as a cook.

2. Work with a partner.

Say the names of the jobs.

a. painter

b. custodian

c. cook

d. clerk

e. mechanic

f. housekeeper

112

Unit 10

PREPARATION

Preteach the new language in the lesson. Follow these suggestions.

● Use pictures or the illustrations in the book to preteach or review the words **painter, custodian, cook, clerk, mechanic,** and **housekeeper.** See "Presenting Recognition Words" on page viii.

● Preteach the dialog. To teach the question **What job do you want?** write the names of jobs on the page on the board. You may wish to include jobs discussed in the Follow-Ups on pages 110–111. Say, *What job do you want?* Have learners repeat. Then point to one of the jobs on the board and say *I want a job as a (job name)* and have learners repeat again. Repeat the procedure with other jobs on the board. Then have

volunteers answer the question about a job they want.

PRESENTATION

 1. Focus attention on the illustration. Have learners say as much as they can about it. You may want to cue them by indicating items for learners to say, or by saying names of items and having learners indicate them. Restate learners' ideas in acceptable English and write them on the board or overhead projector.

Present the dialog. See "Presenting Dialogs" on page viii.

2. Help learners read the directions. Demonstrate by saying the jobs with a volunteer. Then have learners complete the exercise in pairs. Ask volunteers to say the names aloud to the class.

3. Help learners read the directions. Encourage them to say as much as they can about the illustration. Demonstrate by completing the first item on the board or overhead projector. Have learners complete the activity. Check learners' work. Ask volunteers to circle the answers on the board or overhead projector. Ask volunteers to say the words aloud.

4. Help learners read the directions. Demonstrate by completing the first item on the board or overhead projector. Then have learners complete the exercise independently. Check learners' work.

 5. Help learners read the directions. Brainstorm with learners possible answers. Write them on the board or overhead projector.

3. Circle.

Circle PAINTER, CUSTODIAN, HOUSEKEEPER, **and** MECHANIC. **Say the words.**

Department of Employment Services

(PAINTER) WANTED

Riverside Apartments 555-6010

HELP WANTED (HOUSEKEEPER)

Greenway Motel 555-8900

(MECHANIC) WANTED

Rick's Auto Body Shop 555-0734

HELP WANTED (CUSTODIAN)

Chicago Public Schools 555-7711

4. Write.

Write the jobs. Say the jobs.

a. _housekeeper_ _____

b. _custodian_ _____

c. _mechanic_ _____

ON YOUR JOB

5. Complete the sentence.

A What job do you want?

B I want a job as a _____.

6. Work with a partner.

Practice the dialog in 5.

Unit 10

113

Complete the sentence using yourself as an example. Have learners complete the activity. Check learners' work. Then ask volunteers to read their answers aloud.

6. Help learners read the directions. Demonstrate with a volunteer. Take turns asking the question. Then have learners complete the activity in pairs. Have learners switch partners and repeat the exercise. Ask several pairs to say their conversations for the class.

FOLLOW-UP

Name the Job: Write the names of jobs on separate index cards. Pantomime a job and encourage learners to figure out what it is. When they answer correctly, show them the card. Then give cards to

several volunteers. Have learners take turns pantomiming the jobs on the cards while the rest of the class tries to figure them out.

♦ Have each learner write the name of a job on an index card. Then have learners in small groups take turns pantomiming their jobs as the rest of the group tries to figure out each job.

Give one's work experience

Complete a simple job application

★   ★   ★   ★   ★

Application   Experience

1. Practice the dialog.

A I want to apply for the job.
B Do you have any experience?
A Yes, I do. I was a cook from 1995 to 1998.
B OK, please complete this application.

2. Complete the sentence.

I was a _____ from _____ to _____.

3. Write the sentence in 2.

I _____.

I _____.

4. Listen.

Do they have any experience? Circle yes **or** no.

a.	(yes)	no	**b.**	yes	(no)
c.	(yes)	no	**d.**	yes	(no)
e.	yes	(no)	**f.**	(yes)	no

114

Unit 10

SCANS Note

Explain to learners that organizing and maintaining a list of their work experience and/or training is important and useful information to have available when applying for new jobs.

PREPARATION

Preteach the new language in the lesson. Follow these suggestions. See also "Presenting Recognition Words" on page viii.

● Use the word card and Blackline Master 9: Job Application to preteach the recognition word **application.**

● To teach the word **experience,** list a few jobs on the board with time periods for each. Show or draw a picture of a person. For each job on the list say, *From (1996 to 1998) (she) was a (job title).* Indicate the entire list, and say, *This is (her) experience.* Write **experience** above the list.

● Preteach the dialog. To teach **apply,** show learners a real application and say, *I want to apply for a job. I have to complete an application.* Have learners repeat.

PRESENTATION

1. Focus attention on the illustration. Have learners say as much as they can about it. Help learners identify the place and the people. You may want to indicate items in the illustration for learners to say, or say names of items and have learners indicate them. Restate their ideas in acceptable English and write them on the board or overhead projector.

Present the dialog. See "Presenting Dialogs" on page viii.

2. Help learners read the directions. Demonstrate on the board or overhead projector by completing the sentence with personal information. Then have learners work in pairs to complete the sentence. Check

learners' work. Ask volunteers to read their sentences aloud.

3. Help learners read the directions. Demonstrate by copying your sentence on the board. Then have learners complete the activity. Check learners' work.

4. Help learners read the directions. Then present the listening activity. See "Presenting Listening Activities" on page ix. Check learners' work. Ask volunteers to read their answers aloud.

5. Help learners read the directions. Demonstrate by completing the first item on the board or overhead projector. Have learners complete the exercise. Check learners' work. Ask volunteers to say the words aloud.

5. Circle.

Circle Experience **and** Application. **Say the words.**

Job (Application)				
Name: Wendy Chan			Telephone Number: (712) 555-8734	
Address: 2803 Hilltop Lane, Apt. 21, Sacramento, CA 97521				
Work (Experience)				
From	To	Job		Employer
1995	1998	Clerk		Ming Exports
1990	1994	Housekeeper		County Hospital

6. Write.

Look at the application in 5. Answer the questions.

a. When was Wendy Chan a clerk?

<u>   From 1995 to 1998   </u>

b. Where was she a clerk?

<u>   Ming Exports   </u>

 ## 7. Write.

Complete the application.

Job Application				
Name:			Telephone Number:	
Address:				
Work Experience				
From	To	Job		Employer

Unit 10   115

---

6. Help learners read the directions. Ask volunteers to read the questions aloud. Demonstrate by completing the first item on the board or overhead projector. Then have learners complete the activity. Check learners' work. Ask volunteers to say the answers aloud.

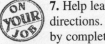 **7.** Help learners read the directions. Demonstrate by completing a sample application on the board or overhead projector. Then have learners complete the activity. Check learners' work.

FOLLOW-UP

Job Experience: Tell learners your job experience. Write the jobs and the time periods on the board or overhead projector. Then arrange learners in pairs to tell each other about their job experience. Model any words learners want to know. Have learners switch partners and repeat the activity. Ask volunteers to repeat their conversations to the class.

◆ Help learners prepare a list of their work experience and/or training. Tell learners to keep the information for reference when they need to fill out applications.

WORKFORCE SKILLS (pages 116–117)

Complete a simple job application

★　　★　　★　　★　　★

Culture Note

Your learners may be reluctant to refuse requests to work nights or weekends. You may want to point out that it is acceptable to turn down certain work shifts or to request alternatives, although workers should give a reason when doing so. You may also want to discuss what reasons are acceptable for turning down certain shifts (family obligations, training conflicts, lack of public transportation, etc.).

| Days | Nights | Weekends |

1. Practice the dialog.

A Can you work nights?
B Yes, I can.
A Can you work weekends?
B No, I can't. I'm sorry.
A When can you start?
B Immediately.
A OK, be here tonight at 5:00.

2. Complete the sentences.

Write days, nights, **or** weekends.

I can work _____.

I can't work _____.

3. Listen.

Circle the word you hear.

a.	days	(nights)	**b.**	nights	(weekends)
c.	(days)	weekends	**d.**	(days)	nights
e.	(nights)	weekends	**f.**	days	(weekends)

116

Unit 10

PREPARATION

Preteach the new language in the lesson. Follow these suggestions.

● Use word cards, picture cards, and a calendar to preteach the recognition words **days, nights,** and **weekends.** See "Presenting Recognition Words" on page viii.

● Preteach the dialog. To teach **can** and **can't,** say, *I can speak English. I can't speak (Russian).* Ask a learner, *Can you speak (learners' native language)?* Help the learner answer *Yes, I can.* Then ask, *Can you speak (a language the learner does not speak)?* Help the learner answer *No, I can't.* Then hold up the picture card and word card for **nights.** Say, *I can work nights.* Have learners repeat. Then show the calendar and point out the weekends. Say, *I can't*

work weekends. Have learners repeat. To teach **immediately,** tell learners you are going to open the door immediately. Then carry out the action very quickly. Ask learners to perform actions such as standing up or opening their books immediately.

PRESENTATION

 1. Focus attention on the illustration. Have learners say as much as they can about it. You may want to cue them by indicating the items for learners to say, or by saying names of items and having learners indicate them. Restate their ideas in acceptable English and write them on the board or overhead projector.

Present the dialog. See "Presenting Dialogs" on page viii.

 2. Help learners read the directions. Demonstrate on the board or overhead projector by completing the first item with personal information. Then have learners complete the sentences. Check learners' work. Ask volunteers to read their sentences aloud.

 3. Help learners read the directions. Then present the listening activity. See "Presenting Listening Activities" on page ix. Check learners' work. Ask volunteers to read their answers aloud.

4. Help learners read the directions. Demonstrate by circling the first item on the board or overhead projector. Have learners complete the activity. Check learners' work.

116

English ASAP

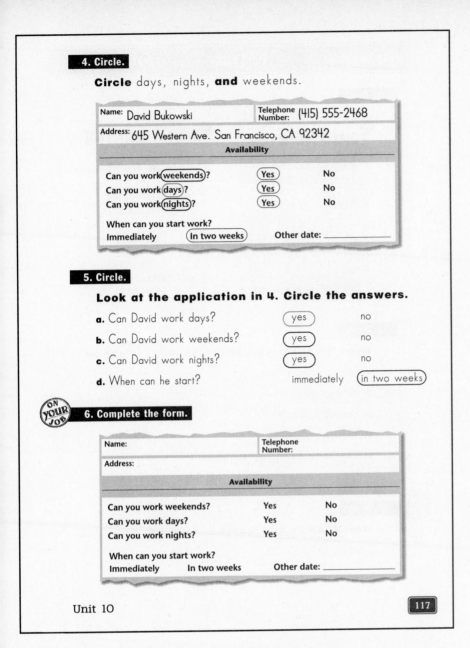

4. Circle.

Circle days, nights, **and** weekends.

Name: David Bukowski	Telephone Number: (415) 555-2468
Address: 645 Western Ave. San Francisco, CA 92342	

Availability

Can you work (weekends)? (Yes) No
Can you work (days)? (Yes) No
Can you work (nights)? (Yes) No

When can you start work?
Immediately (In two weeks) Other date: _____

5. Circle.

Look at the application in 4. Circle the answers.

a. Can David work days? (yes) no
b. Can David work weekends? (yes) no
c. Can David work nights? (yes) no
d. When can he start? immediately (in two weeks)

 6. Complete the form.

Name:	Telephone Number:
Address:	

Availability

Can you work weekends? Yes No
Can you work days? Yes No
Can you work nights? Yes No

When can you start work?
Immediately In two weeks Other date: _____

Unit 10

117

5. Help learners read the directions. Demonstrate by completing the first item on the board or overhead projector. Then have learners complete the activity. Check learners' work. Ask volunteers to say their answers aloud and indicate an appropriate picture card or days on the calendar.

 6. Help learners read the directions. Complete a sample form on the board or overhead projector. Then have learners complete the form. Check learners' work. Ask volunteers to read their answers aloud and indicate appropriate picture cards or days on the calendar.

FOLLOW-UP

When Can You Work? Survey your class to find out how many learners can work days, nights, and/or weekends. Write the numbers on the board under the appropriate headings.

♦ Help learners brainstorm names of jobs people might do in each of these time periods. List them under the appropriate headings.

Identify kinds of jobs

Read help-wanted ads and signs

Complete a simple job application

★   ★   ★   ★   ★

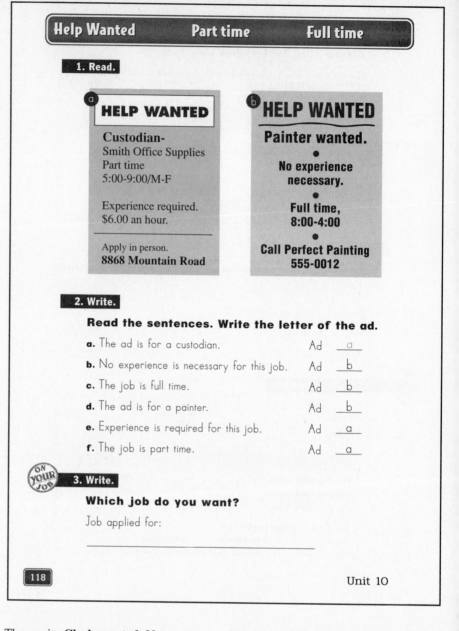

Help Wanted   Part time   Full time

1. Read.

(a) HELP WANTED

Custodian-
Smith Office Supplies
Part time
5:00-9:00/M-F

Experience required.
$6.00 an hour.

Apply in person.
8868 Mountain Road

(b) HELP WANTED

Painter wanted.
•
**No experience
necessary.**
•
**Full time,
8:00-4:00**
•
**Call Perfect Painting
555-0012**

2. Write.

Read the sentences. Write the letter of the ad.

a. The ad is for a custodian.   Ad __a__

b. No experience is necessary for this job.   Ad __b__

c. The job is full time.   Ad __b__

d. The ad is for a painter.   Ad __b__

e. Experience is required for this job.   Ad __a__

f. The job is part time.   Ad __a__

3. Write.

Which job do you want?

Job applied for:

_____

118   Unit 10

Language Note

*You may want to point out that other words and phrases that indicate job openings include (**job title**) **Needed**, **Looking for** (**job title**), **Openings for** (**job title**), and **Position Available**.*

PREPARATION

Preteach the new language in the lesson. Follow these suggestions.

• Use word cards, the help-wanted section of a newspaper, and/or the illustrations in the book to preteach the recognition words **help wanted, part time,** and **full time.** (You may want to enlarge part of the help-wanted section of the newspaper on a photocopier so learners can see it easily.) See "Presenting Recognition Words" on page viii.

• Teach **Experience required** by writing **Painter wanted. Experience required.** on the board. Hold up a picture of a painter and say, *He was a painter from 1993 to 1998. He can get this job.* Hold up a picture of another person and say, *He was a cook. He wasn't a painter. He can't get this job.*

Then write **Clerk wanted. No experience required.** Ask whether both people can get the job.

PRESENTATION

1. Focus attention on the help-wanted signs. Have learners say as much as they can about them.

2. Help learners read the directions. Demonstrate by completing the first item on the board or overhead projector. Have learners complete the activity. Check learners' work. Ask volunteers to read the answers aloud.

 3. Help learners read the directions. Complete the activity yourself as an example. Brainstorm with the class job choices other than those listed on the signs. Write them on the board or overhead projector.

Then have learners complete the activity. Ask volunteers to read their answers to the class.

4. Help learners read the directions. Demonstrate by completing the first item on the board or overhead projector. Then have learners complete the activity. Check learners' work. Have volunteers circle the correct answers on the board or overhead projector and say the words.

5. Help learners read the directions. Demonstrate by completing the application on the board or overhead projector. Then have learners complete the activity independently. Check learners' work. Ask several volunteers to read their answers to the class.

English ASAP

4. Circle.

Circle HELP WANTED, Full time, Part time, Experience, **and** experience. **Say the words.**

HELP WANTED

COOK WANTED.
(Experience) required.
(Full time) weekends and nights.
$8.00 an hour.
Tasty Plate Diner, 37 Stuart Street

HELP WANTED

HOUSEKEEPER
No (experience) necessary.
(Part time) days.
$5.75 an hour.
Call Mercy Hospital: 555-0301

---

5. Write.

Apply for a job in 4. Complete the application.

Availability		
Job applied for: _____		
When can you start work?		
Immediately In two weeks	Other date: _____	
Can you work weekends?	Yes	No
Can you work days?	Yes	No
Can you work nights?	Yes	No

Unit 10   119

FOLLOW-UP

Filling Out Job Applications: Bring in help-wanted ads from your community's newspaper for jobs your learners might be interested in. (You might enlarge them on a photocopier so learners can read them easily.) Have each learner find a job he or she might like to apply for. Ask learners to fill out applications for the jobs they want. Use Blackline Master 9: Job Application. Model any words learners might want to know. Check learners' work.

♦ Arrange learners in small groups. Have them show each other the help-wanted ads with the jobs they applied for, and read their applications aloud.

Extension

1. Circle.

Look at the ads. Circle the job you want.

Mechanic needed-	**Painter-**
Joe's Car Repair	Dale's Painting Service
Full time position.	Part time position.
$13.00 an hour.	Experience preferred.
Experience required.	$9.00 an hour.
7 Unity Street.	Call 555-2018.

2. Write.

Complete the application.

JOB APPLICATION		
Name: _____		Telephone Number:
Address: _____		
_____		Position Applied For:
_____		

WORK EXPERIENCE			
From	To	Job	Employer

AVAILABILITY		
Can you work days? ❑ Yes ❑ No		When can you start work?
Can you work nights? ❑ Yes ❑ No		❑ Immediately
Can you work weekends? ❑ Yes ❑ No		❑ In two weeks

120   Unit 10

Language Note

*Explain to learners that the word **position** can have the same meaning as **job**.*

PREPARATION

Review the new language using the following suggestions.

● On the board or overhead projector, write the words **mechanic** and **painter.** Ask volunteers to say the words aloud and find a matching picture card or illustration in the book for each job.

● To review **part time** and **full time,** write some work schedules on the board, such as **8-2, M-W** and **9-5, M-F.** Have learners say whether the schedules are part time or full time.

● To review **application** and **experience,** follow the procedures on page 114.

● Use a calendar and picture and word cards to review **days, nights,** and **weekends.**

PRESENTATION

1. Help learners read the directions. Demonstrate by telling learners which job you want and circling it on the board or overhead projector. Then have learners circle their choices.

2. Help learners read the directions. Demonstrate by filling in the first few items of the application on the board or overhead projector. Then have learners fill in the application. Check learners' work.

FOLLOW-UP

Job Interview: To prepare learners for job interviews, role-play a job interview with a volunteer as the rest of the class watches. When the interview is complete, ask the class to repeat the questions you asked. Write the questions on the board or overhead projector.

♦ Have learners use the list of questions to role-play job interviews in pairs. Ask volunteers to repeat their interviews for the class.

1. Write.

Complete the application.

MERCY HOSPITAL	APPLICATION FOR EMPLOYMENT

Name: _____   Telephone Number: _____

Address: _____

City: _____   State: _____   Zip Code: _____

Position Applied For: _____

When can you start?   ☐ Immediately   ☐ In two weeks
When can you work?   ☐ Days   ☐ Nights   ☐ Weekends

WORK EXPERIENCE			
From	To	Job	Employer

2. Circle.

Read the sentences. Circle the ad.

ⓐ MECHANIC WANTED

Good Wrench Garage
$12 an hour, full-time.
Experience required.

ⓑ COOK WANTED

Sandy's Hamburgers
Part time, $7.50 an hour.
No experience required.

1. The ad is for a mechanic.   (Ad a)   Ad b

2. The job is part time.   Ad a   (Ad b)

3. Experience is required for this job. (Ad a)   Ad b

4. The ad is for a cook.   Ad a   (Ad b)

Unit 10   121

ASAP PROJECT

You may want to help learners set up "employment agencies" at several places around the room. At each, display a variety of help-wanted ads that would be of interest to your learners (or have learners write help-wanted ads for jobs that they would like to have). Ask for volunteers to serve as "clerks" at the agencies. Ask the rest of the learners to visit the agencies and ask questions about the jobs they see posted. Provide clerks with copies of Blackline Master 9: Job Application. The clerk can hand an application to each learner who visits the agency and wants to apply for a job. Learners can fill them out for the job they are interested in. Check learners' applications. As an extension of this activity, you might arrange for your class to visit a local employment office, or for an interviewer to visit your classroom.

PREPARATION

Briefly review the new language before learners open their books. Write the words on the board or overhead projector and ask volunteers to find the matching picture cards or to indicate appropriate illustrations in their books.

Use Blackline Master 9: Job Application to help learners review how to fill out a job application.

Provide specific help as needed until you are sure learners feel confident that they know all the new words and language.

PRESENTATION

Use any of the procedures in "Evaluation," page ix, with this page. Record individuals' results on the Unit 10 Individual Competency Chart. Record the class's results on the Class Cumulative Competency Chart.

INFORMAL WORKPLACE-SPECIFIC ASSESSMENT

Ask learners to complete a real job application for a job they want.

 # Listening Transcript

Page 5

Exercise 4. Listen.

Circle the word you hear.

a. A: What's your last name?
    B: My last name's Reyna. R-E-Y-N-A.

b. A: What's her name?
    B: Her name's Eva.

c. A: Please write your last name on
        the form.
    B: Excuse me?
    A: Please write your last name.

d. A: Tell me your first name again,
        please.
    B: My first name's Leonard.
    A: Nice to meet you, Leonard.

Page 6

Exercise 3. Listen.

Circle the word you hear.

a. A: What's your address?
    B: My address is 42 River Street.

b. A: What number building does Gloria
        work in?
    B: Number 307.

c. A: What street is the warehouse on?
    B: I think it's on Water Street.

d. A: Do you know the address of the
        eye clinic?
    B: Yes, the address is 22 Lakeshore
        Drive. It's next to the hospital.

Page 8

Exercise 3. Listen.

Circle the words you hear.

a. A: What state are we shipping this
        package to?
    B: The state? California.

b. A: Do you know the zip code?
    B: The zip code is 93365.

c. A: What city are you flying from?
    B: Miami.
    A: And what city are you flying to?
    B: New York.

Page 10

Exercise 3. Listen.

Do you hear *telephone number?*
Circle *yes* or *no*.

a. A: What's Arthur's telephone number?
    B: I don't know his telephone number,
        but I can look it up for you.

b. A: What's the address for our next
        delivery?
    B: 18 Main Street.

c. A: Do you have the telephone number
        for Apex Shoe Repair?
    B: Wait a minute. I have it right here.
        It's 555-6767.

d. A: In order to complete this job
        application, we'll need your telephone
        number.
    B: I don't have a telephone right now,
        but I can give you my uncle's
        telephone number if that's all right.
    A: Of course. That'll be fine.

e. A: Is there a telephone number where we
        can reach you in case of emergency?
    B: Yes, the telephone number is
        555-1267.
    A: Thanks.

f. A: The pet clinic is on Town Road.
    B: What number?
    A: Number fourteen.

Page 16

Exercise 3. Listen.

Circle the place you hear.

a. A: I'm here to paint Mr. Higgins' office. Can you tell me where it is?
   B: Mr. Higgins' office? It's over there on the right.

b. A: We need to move these tables to the break room.
   B: That should be easy to do. The break room isn't far.

c. A: Excuse me. Do you know where the exit is?
   B: Yes, the exit's at the end of the hall, on the left.
   A: On the left? Thanks.

d. A: I can't find the ladies' room on this map.
   B: There's a ladies' room straight ahead on the right and another one on the second floor.
   A: Thanks.

Page 18

Exercise 3. Listen.

Circle the word you hear.

a. A: Where do you want me to hang this poster?
   B: On the right.
   A: On the right near the window?
   B: Yes, that'll be fine.

b. A: Where are the pay phones?
   B: They're down the hall on the left.
   A: On the left. Thanks.

c. A: Is the break room up ahead on the left?
   B: Yes, it's on the left, next to room 25.

d. A: Where's the exit?
   B: It's on the right, just past the soda machines. You can't miss it.

Page 20

Exercise 3. Listen.

Do you hear *supply room*? Circle *yes* or *no*.

a. A: We're out of garbage bags. Are there any in the supply room?

B: Yes, there are. Do you want me to get some for you?

b. A: Could you bring me some sponges from the supply room?
   B: Sure, how many?
   A: Oh, about half a dozen.

c. A: Take these towels to the cafeteria as soon as you can.
   B: Sure, I'll do it right away.

Page 22

Exercise 3. Listen.

Look at the picture in 1. Circle *yes* or *no*.

a. A: I need some large bags.
   B: Bags are on the top shelf. I can get them for you.

b. A: I'm looking for some notebooks.
   B: All the notebooks are on the middle shelf. See them over there?
   A: Yes, I do. On the middle shelf.

c. A: Can you help me? I need the towels, but they're on the top shelf and I can't reach that high.
   B: Sure, I can help you. How many towels do you need?

d. A: Are there any envelopes in here?
   B: Yes, there's a box of envelopes on the top shelf.
   A: Are you sure?

e. A: Where are the gloves?
   B: Look on the bottom shelf. I just put some there.
   A: OK, thanks.

f. A: Do you know where the paper is?
   B: Yes, there's paper on the bottom shelf.
   A: On the bottom shelf? You're right.

Page 28

Exercise 3. Listen.

Circle the word you hear.

a. A: I can't pull this cord.
   B: You need to unlock the safety latch. Then you should be able to pull it easily.

b. A: Which button do I push to start the scanner?
   B: Push this button to start. Push the button next to it to stop.

c. A: How do I put this in reverse?
   B: Turn the key. Then push down on the pedal.

d. A: I can't get this sewing machine to start. Can you help me?
   B: Sure. Before you can start this machine, you have to pull the lever.
   A: Oh, I see. Thanks.

e. A: Marty wants us to take this cart back to housekeeping.
   B: All right, I'll pull it if you get the door.

f. A: Help me push this desk over by the wall.
   B: Sure, I'll be right there.

Page 30

Exercise 3. Listen.

Circle the word you hear.

a. A: Is the dishwasher on?
   B: Yes, I already turned it on.

b. A: This coffee is cold. Did someone turn off the coffee maker?
   B: I don't know, but I can check.

c. A: How do I turn off this dryer?
   B: Push STOP. That's the small button on the back.

d. Please read the manual before you start that sander. I don't want any accidents.

e. A: I can't get the microwave oven to start.
   B: Did you check to see if it's plugged in?
   A: No, I didn't, but I will now.

f. A: Can you turn off the vacuum cleaner for a minute? I think I hear the telephone ringing.

B: Of course I'll turn it off.
A: Thanks.

Page 32

Exercise 3. Listen.

Circle the words you hear.

a. A: How do I replace the bag for this vacuum cleaner?
   B: Take out the old bag. Close the top securely.

b. A: Where do I put in the toner?
   B: Open the door to the copier. Put the toner in here.

c. A: I can't get this machine to start.
   B: Put in the key all the way.
   A: I did that.
   B: Now turn it to the left.

d. A: The green light on the coffee maker just went on. What should I do?
   B: Take out the pot. It's ready to serve.

e. A: How do I get into this computer program?
   B: You need to put in your password. Then press ENTER.

f. A: Should I take out the cake?
   B: No, don't take it out yet. It should bake a little longer.

Page 34

Exercise 3. Listen.

Circle the word you hear.

a. A: Can I close the trunk now?
   B: No, wait a minute. I need to get the tool kit out first. Then you can close it.

b. A: I need you to close the freezer door for me. My hands are full.
   B: No problem. I'll close it for you.

c. A: Do you know how to open the door?
   B: Yes, just put your ID card on the sensor. The door will open automatically.

d. A: I can't open this gate. Do you know how?

Listening Transcript

B: Uh-huh. Push this button. See? Now you can open it.

Page 40

Exercise 3. Listen.

Circle the day you hear.

a. A: Can you work late this Thursday?
B: No, not this week. I've got a doctor's appointment on Thursday.

b. It feels as if Friday's always our busiest day. I think I make more deliveries on Friday than any other day of the week.

c. A: My son's playing football on Saturday. Can you come to the game?
B: What time does the game start? I work on Saturday morning.
A: At 2:00.
B: Sure, I'll be there.

d. A: Do you know when we get paid next?
B: On Tuesday.
A: Tuesday? Thanks.

Page 42

Exercise 3. Listen.

Circle the date you hear.

a. A: When can I see the dentist?
B: How's November 10?
A: November 10 isn't good for me. Is there anything available the next week?

b. A: When can you start work?
B: How's next Monday?
A: December 13? That'll be fine.
B: Good, I'll see you on December 13.

c. A: They're installing the new irrigation system on June 25.
B: June 25 is next Thursday. I didn't realize they were starting work so soon.

d. A: Can you work for me next Wednesday?
B: July 14?
A: Yes.
B: Sure, I'm free on the fourteenth. I'd be happy to help you out.

Page 44

Exercise 3. Listen.

Circle the year you hear.

a. A: Did you start work here in 1997?
B: Yes, I started on March 30, 1997.

b. A: When did you arrive in the United States?
B: In 1989.
A: When exactly?
B: On July 2, 1989.

c. A: When will you finish your apprentice work?
B: In September 2001.
A: Was that 2001?
B: Yes, and I'm really looking forward to it.

d. A: Just fill in your date of birth and your application form will be complete.
B: Oh, OK. It's August 10, 1982.

Page 47

Exercise 3. Listen.

Circle the time you hear.

a. A: Excuse me. When does the next train arrive?
B: It should be here at 4:00.
A: 4:00? Thanks.

b. A: Wake up! It's 7:30. It's time to get ready for work.
B: 7:30? Oh, no! I'm late.

c. A: Do you want to meet for lunch today around 12:15?
B: 12:15's OK. See you then.

d. A: What time should we turn on the lights tonight?
B: How about 5:45?
A: 5:45 sounds right to me.

UNIT 5

Page 53

Exercise 3. Listen.

Circle the words you hear.

a. A: Welcome to Nemo's Pizza Shop. May I take your order?
   B: Yes, please. I'd like a large pizza to go.

b. A: Thank you. Here's your change.
   B: I think you still owe me a dollar.
   A: Oh, you're right. Here you are.
   B: Thank you.

c. A: Hello, Northern Construction Company. How may I direct your call?
   B: I'd like to speak to Bill Smith.
   A: One moment, please.

d. A: Thank you for calling Quick Copiers. This is Norman. How can I help you?
   B: I'm calling from Cole Manufacturing. We're having problems with our new copier.
   A: I'll put your call through to our service department.

Page 55

Exercise 3. Listen.

Do you hear *Customer Service?*
Circle *yes* or *no.*

a. I bought this ceiling fan here yesterday, and I'm having trouble getting it to work. I'd like to exchange it. Can you tell me where the customer service department is?

b. A: May I help you?
   B: I think so. The starter on this mower isn't working correctly.
   A: Let me call my manager. He can help you with that.

c. A: Is there something I can do for you?
   B: I'd like to return this microwave oven.
   A: Customer Service takes care of all returns. Just walk straight ahead to the back of the store.
   B: Thanks.

d. A: Can I help you?
   B: There's something wrong with this battery. It won't take a charge.
   A: You need to go to Customer Service. Someone there can take care of you.

Page 56

Exercise 3. Listen.

Circle the word you hear.

a. A: Do you know how much these boxes are? There's no price on them.
   B: I'm sorry. Let me check on that for you.

b. A: Excuse me. This coffee has milk and sugar in it. I asked for it black.
   B: I'm sorry, ma'am. I'll get you a fresh cup of black coffee right away.
   A: Thank you.

c. A: I've enjoyed talking to you about job opportunities. Goodbye and thank you.
   B: It was my pleasure, George. Good luck in your job hunt.

d. A: This is Ernest Chang in room 508. There aren't any towels in the bathroom.
   B: I'm sorry, Mr. Chang. I'll send someone up with towels right away.

Page 58

Exercise 3. Listen.

Circle the word you hear.

a. A: Would you like to return these speakers?
   B: Yes, I would. And I'd like a refund, please.
   A: Just complete this form and I can give you your refund.

b. A: This can opener doesn't work. I'd like to exchange it for a new one.
   B: I'd be happy to exchange it for you. Do you have the receipt?
   A: Yes, I've got the receipt right here.

c. A: I've got to return this ladder. Can I get a refund for it?

Listening Transcript

B: Of course you can. Just fill out and sign this form.

d. A: Good morning.
B: Good morning. I'd like to exchange these gloves for a smaller size.
A: OK, I can exchange those gloves for you. What size do you need?

UNIT 6

Page 64

Exercise 3. Listen.

Circle the words you hear.

a. A: What time do I have to come in tomorrow, Rita?
B: Let me check the appointment book. . . .You've got a cut and color at 8:00.
A: OK, I'll be in early.

b. A: Hello, Family Bakery.
B: Hi, Martha. This is Rasheed. My dentist appointment was canceled, so I'll be in on time today.
A: Good. Thanks for calling, Rasheed.

c. A: Good morning, Uptown Catering.
B: Dorothy? This is Bill Gordon. I'm sorry, but I'm going to be late today. My car won't start. I should be there in about 25 minutes.
A: OK, Bill. See you then.

d. A: This is Carey Miller. I can't come to the phone right now, but please leave me a message and I'll return your call as soon as possible. Thank you.
B: Hi, Carey. This is Antonio. Can you cover for me at the restaurant Monday afternoon? I need to pick up my daughter at day care, and I might be a little late. Give me a call. My number's 555-4336. Thanks.

Page 66

Exercise 3. Listen.

Do you hear *repeat?* Circle *yes* or *no*.

a. A: The telephone number at the training center is 555-9288.
B: Can you repeat that?
A: Sure, it's 555-9288.

b. A: I need 100 copies of this report for the staff meeting this afternoon.
B: OK, I'll get started on them now.
A: Thank you.

c. A: Jack up the car and rotate the tires.
B: I'm sorry. What did you say?
A: Wait a minute. I'll show you.

d. A: You're in charge of cleaning rooms 102 and 108.
B: Which rooms? Could you repeat the numbers?
A: Sure, 102 and 108.

e. A: The meeting is at 12:30 in the board room.
B: OK, I'll tell the others.
A: Thanks.

f. A: Where are we taking this order?
B: 88 East Eighth Street.
A: Excuse me?
B: I'm sorry. That is kind of confusing. Let me repeat that for you. It's 88 East Eighth Street.

Page 70

Exercise 3. Listen.

Circle the word you hear.

a. A: Emilio, how do you get to work so early?
B: I take the express bus.

b. A: How do you come to work?
B: I walk almost every day. I live near here and, of course, it's great exercise.

c. A: Can you drive me to the store tomorrow?
B: I'm sorry. I can't. My car's in the shop getting fixed.

d. If we want to take the bus, we'd better hurry. It leaves in ten minutes.

e. A: I'm calling about the ad for a delivery person.
B: Can you drive a truck?
A: Yes, I can.

B: Good. Would you like to come in later today for an interview?

f. A: It's a beautiful day. Let's walk downtown for a change.
   B: OK, walking sounds like fun.

Page 76

Exercise 3. Listen.

Circle the amount you hear.

a. A: Will that be cash or check?
   B: What was the total again?
   A: $21.90.
   B: $21.90? I think I'll pay cash.

b. A: This paint is on sale for $15.10.
   B: $15.10? That's not much of a sale.

c. A: All together that comes to $13.60.
   B: $13.60? Will you take a check for that?

d. A: I think you gave me too much change. I should get $7.40 back.
   B: You're right. Thank you. Your change should be $7.40.

e. A: The work boots in this catalog are $65.00 a pair.
   B: Oh, I didn't know that work boots cost $65.00.

f. A: The electric bill this month was $32.88.
   B: $32.88? That's less than it was last month.

Page 79

Exercise 3. Listen.

Write *cash* or *check*.

a. A: How much is a case of cat food?
   B: $15.95.
   A: $15.95? I guess I'll pay for that in cash.

b. A: Your total comes to $21.50. How would you like to pay?
   B: Can I write a check?
   A: Yes, but I'll need to see some ID.

c. A: I'm sorry. We only accept cash.
   B: OK, I think I have enough cash with me. What was the total again?

d. A: Harold's requires a 20% deposit on all layaways.
   B: Will you accept a check for that?
   A: A check will be fine.

Page 81

Exercise 3. Listen.

Do they ask for ID? Circle *yes* or *no*.

a. A: I'll need to see some ID, please.
   B: Some ID? Here's my driver's license.

b. Please complete this application, sign it, and bring it back to me when you're done.

c. A: Did you sign the check?
   B: Yes, I signed the check and wrote my account number on the back.

d. A: May I see your ID?
   B: Yes, here's my passport.

Page 83

Exercise 3. Listen.

Do you hear *deposit*? Circle *yes* or *no*.

a. A: I'd like to deposit this check.
   B: OK, please fill out this deposit slip.

b. A: Has my deposit of $362.44 cleared yet?
   B: Yes, that deposit cleared yesterday.

c. A: Will that be cash, check, or charge?
   B: Check. What was the total again?
   A: All together it came to $25.32.

d. A: Do you want to deposit this to your checking or savings account?
   B: Savings, please.
   A: OK, then you need to fill out this deposit slip.

e. A: Did you deposit your paycheck yet?
   B: No, not yet. I was going to deposit it on my way home today.

f. A: May I help you?

B: I'd like to cash this check.
A: Do you have an account with this bank?
B: Yes, I do.

Page 85

Circle the amount you hear.

a. A: If we change the oil and replace the windshield wipers, it'll cost you $27.98.
    B: $27.98? OK, go ahead and do it.

b. A: All the winter coats are now $48.00.
    B: Men's and women's coats?
    A: Yes, mark them all $48.00.

c. A: How much extra would it cost to send this package overnight?
    B: $14.10.
    A: $14.10's kind of high. I'll send it regular mail.

d. A: All together the calendars you ordered come to $55.15.
    B: You'll take a purchase order for $55.15, won't you?

e. A: Jack needs to be more careful when he's working. It cost $30.25 to replace that broken window.
    B: Only $30.25? I thought it'd be more than that.

f. A: Here's your change. $11.11.
    B: Are you sure that's correct?
    A: Let me check. . . .Yes, ma'am. $11.11's your change.

Page 88

Circle the word you hear.

a. A: What happened?
    B: He slipped on the wet floor.
    A: Is he OK?
    B: No, he isn't. He hurt his arm. I think we should take him to the emergency room.

b. A: What's the matter with your hand?
    B: I cut it on this glass. It hurts a little.
    A: It's not a bad cut. I'll wash it and put on a bandage.

c. A: The doctor says my arm is broken.
    B: What happened?
    A: I was carrying a lot of heavy boxes, and I wasn't watching where I was going.

d. A: What's the problem?
    B: My back hurts.
    A: How long has it hurt?
    B: For a few days now.

Page 90

Circle the words you hear.

a. A: You can't smoke in here.
    B: Why not?
    A: The sign says NO SMOKING.

b. A: Be careful with that box. It contains poison.
    B: You know, this box really should be labeled more carefully.

c. A: Watch out! Didn't you see the DANGER sign?
    B: No, I didn't. Thanks for the warning.

d. A: Did you see the NO SMOKING sign?
    B: No, I didn't, but I'm glad they put one up. Someone could start a fire here very easily.

e. A: That barrel contains poison, so be careful when you move it.
    B: Good point. I'd better put on my safety gear.

f. Make sure no one goes in that door marked DANGER. They're doing some testing in there right now.

Page 92

Circle the word you hear.

a. A: There's a fire in the kitchen!
    B: A fire? Call 911!

b. A: I'd like to report an accident.
B: What's the location?
A: The accident's in front of 19 Sergeant Street.
B: We'll send help right away.

c. A: Is that the fire alarm?
B: Yes, it is. And I smell smoke.
A: Let's get out of the building now!

d. A: There's been an accident.
B: What happened?
A: Gino fell down the stairs. There's an ambulance on its way.

e. A: Where's the accident?
B: On Broad Street. A car ran a red light.
A: Broad Street? We can be there in five minutes.

f. A: Has anyone shown you where the fire exits are?
B: No, not yet.

Page 95

Exercise 3. Listen.

What do the people do? Circle.

a. A: John burned his hand.
B: I think he needs to go to the hospital. City Hospital isn't far and I can drive.

b. A: She's unconscious. Call 911 right away.
B: I already called 911. They're sending an ambulance.

c. A: Lisa fell and hit her head. What should we do?
B: Don't move her. I'll call 911.

d. A: Christy just fainted. Do you think she needs to go to the hospital?
B: Yes, I do. I think a doctor should look at her.

UNIT 9
Page 101

Exercise 3. Listen.

Circle the word you hear.

a. A: Excuse me. I'm looking for the supervisor.
B: That would be Susan. She's over there by the door.
A: Thanks.

b. A: Have you met your coworkers yet?
B: My coworkers? No, I haven't met them.
A: OK, let me take you around and introduce you to them.

c. A: I'm not sure what I should do now.
B: I think your coworkers are loading the trucks over there.
A: Thanks.

d. A: Did you find out what to do?
B: No, we haven't.
A: Your supervisor should have the work orders.
B: I'll go find him. Do you know where he is?

Page 103

Exercise 3. Listen.

Do you hear *Nice to meet you*?
Circle *yes* or *no*.

a. A: Pedro, this is Sandra.
B: Nice to meet you, Sandra.
C: Nice to meet you, Pedro.

b. Hi, Ming. I'm Julia. It's nice to meet you. I've heard a lot of good things about you from your boss at the warehouse.

c. A: I don't think we've met. I'm Steve.
B: Nice to meet you, Steve. I'm Katya. I'm so glad to be working here at the shelter. What can I do to get started?

d. A: Where are you from, Carmen?
B: I'm from Houston.
A: Oh, really? I'm from Houston, too.

Page 105

Exercise 3. Listen.

Circle the words you hear.

a. A: Karen, when's our afternoon break?
B: 2:30.

A: 2:30? Good. That's only a few
minutes from now.

b. A: All of the employees in this
division get a morning break at
9:30.
B: So everyone takes their morning
break at the same time?
A: That's right.

c. A: Do we get a break in the afternoon?
B: Yes, there's an afternoon break at
3:00.
A: OK, do you want to meet then?

d. Can I take an early lunch today? I'd
like to go to my daughter's school
and have lunch with her.

Page 107

Exercise 3. Listen.

Do you hear *Good work?* Circle *yes* or *no*.

a. A: Did you work on these dresses?
B: Yes, I did.
A: They look beautiful. Good work.
B: Thank you, Ms. Phillips.

b. A: Please wash these glasses again,
Jill. They have spots on them.
B: I'm sorry. I'll wash them now.

c. A: Good work on painting this room,
Ken.
B: Thanks, I'll tell Eddie you said so.
He was a real help to me on this job.

d. A: You finished these reports early?
Good work, Mary.
B: Thank you, Ms. Kelly.

Page 114

Exercise 4. Listen.

Do they have any experience?
Circle *yes* or *no*.

a. A: I'm calling about the ad for a
gardener.
B: Do you have any experience?
A: Yes, before I came to this country,
I was a gardener for many years.
B: Good. Can you come in later today

for an interview?
A: Sure.

b. A: General Hospital. May I help you?
B: Yes, I saw your ad for a
housekeeper. I'd like to apply for
the job. Can you tell me about it?
A: Well, it's a part time position, and
the salary's $6.25 an hour. Do you
have any experience?
B: No, I don't. Is that a problem?
A: No, it's OK. Experience isn't
required. We have a training
program for people without
experience.
B: That sounds great.

c. A: Look at this ad, May. It's a perfect
job for you.
B: What kind of job is it?
A: The American Cafe's looking for
a full time cook with experience
working in a restaurant.
B: That sounds perfect. I have three
years of experience working at
the Pickwick Restaurant. Is there
a phone number I can call?
A: Here.

d. A: I'm interested in applying for the
clerk's job.
B: Tell me, do you have any
experience?
A: No, I don't have experience as a
clerk, but I'm very organized and I
enjoy office work.
B: All right, please fill out this form.
A: Thank you.

e. A: Hello, I'm here about your ad for
a painter.
B: Do you have experience as a
painter?
A: No, I don't have any experience,
but I want to learn.
B: Well, that's OK. We prefer
experience but don't require it.

f. A: I need to find a job.
B: Here's a Help Wanted ad for a
custodian.
A: Really? I have experience as a
custodian. Who's the job with?
B: The city school system. They want
people with experience, so it sounds
like a good job for you.

Page 116

Circle the word you hear.

a. A: We need a cook who can work
        nights.
    B: I can work nights.
    A: That's good. Could you start Friday
        night?
    B: Yes, Friday night's fine.

b. A: Why do you want to work weekends?
    B: I go to school, so weekends are the
        best time for me to work.
    A: Oh, you're a student. We hire a lot
        of students.

c. A: Look, John, this ad is for a mechanic
        who can work days from nine to
        five.
    B: Days from nine to five? That's just
        what I'm looking for.
    A: Here's the ad.
    B: Thanks, I'll call them right away.

d. A: Do you have any positions open
        that are days only?
    B: Yes, we do. This is the list of posi-
        tions that are days only.
    A: May I have a look at that?
    B: Certainly. Here you are.

e. A: Can you work nights?
    B: Yes, that's fine.
    A: Oh, good. We have a hard time
        finding people who can work
        nights.

f. A: The only time I can't work is on
        weekends.
    B: Actually, we're not open on week-
        ends, so that's not a problem. Can
        you start this week?
    A: Sure thing.

The blackline masters on pages 137–149 allow for additional reinforcement and enrichment. Because you can make as many copies as you need, you can use them for a variety of purposes throughout the book:

• Use Blackline Masters 1–5 to present or reinforce basic literacy skills.

• Learners who complete individual, pair, or small group activities before the rest of the class can complete a Blackline Master activity independently.

• In open-entry/open-exit programs, use the Blackline Masters to provide any needed review as new learners join the class.

• Use the Blackline Masters as games or for pair work.

• Use a Blackline Master activity as review before the Performance Check page.

• Assign them as homework.

Here are a few specific suggestions on ways you can use each Blackline Master. Feel free to think of additional activities of your own.

Blackline Master 1: Top-to-Bottom and Left-to-Right Progression

• Draw the dotted line and staircase on the board or overhead projector and demonstrate tracing the line with your finger or a pencil. Then have learners start at the arrow and trace the dotted line on a copy of the Blackline Master with their fingers and/or with their pencils. Then have them trace the line in the air with their fingers and/or with their pencils. Finally, have learners follow the line with their eyes only.

Blackline Masters 2–3: Alphabet

• Blackline Masters 2–3 can be presented before beginning Unit 1, and/or they can be used for reinforcement as the letters are taught within the units. Introduce the letters, three at a time. Use flash cards to identify each letter. Hold up the flash card and say the letter. Have learners repeat. Point out the differences between the capital and the lower-case letters. Have

learners open their books and trace the target letters with their fingers. Suggest that they follow the direction of the arrows. Then have them trace the letters with their pencils. You may also ask them to trace the letters in the air with their fingers or pencils. Demonstrate copying the letters on the board or overhead projector. Then have learners copy the letters. Check each learner's work and provide immediate feedback. For additional reinforcement, use Blackline Master 5: Lined Paper.

Blackline Master 4: Numbers

• Introduce the numerals, three at a time. Use flash cards to identify each number. Hold up the flash card and say the number. Have learners repeat. Have learners open their books and trace the target numbers with their fingers. Suggest that they follow the directions of the arrows. Then have them trace the numbers with their pencils. You may also ask them to trace the numbers in the air with their fingers or pencils. Demonstrate copying the numbers on the board or overhead projector. Then have learners copy the numbers. Check each learner's work and provide immediate feedback. For additional reinforcement, use Blackline Master 5: Lined Paper.

Blackline Master 5: Lined Paper

• Duplicate as needed to provide learners with writing paper for extra practice in writing letters, numbers, words, and sentences.

Blackline Masters 6-7: Common Directions

• Use these blackline masters to clarify the directions on the Student Book pages. Read each direction aloud. Have learners repeat. Use the illustration on the page and pantomime where possible to demonstrate meaning. Then say the direction and have learners act it out. When you have taught all the directions, say them in and out of order and have learners act them out.

Blackline Master 8: Identification Forms

- To help learners generalize that different identification forms ask for the same information, have learners look at both forms. Say **name** and have learners point to it on both forms. Continue with other items on the forms.

- Have learners fill out the forms independently.

- Have pairs interview each other and complete one of the forms for their partners.

Blackline Master 9: Job Application

- Have learners complete the application about themselves. Then collect the completed applications, check them, and return them to learners with another copy of the application. Have them complete the second application with the corrected information. Check their work. Remind them to carry this application with them when applying for jobs to help them complete the applications quickly and accurately.

- Have pairs interview each other and complete the application for their partners.

Blackline Master 10: Telephone

- Have learners practice dialing telephone numbers. Say telephone numbers aloud and have learners touch the numbers on the keypad. Use the numbers of businesses, service agencies, long distance numbers, 800 and 888 numbers, 911, directory assistance, the school's office or attendance office, learners' employers (for reporting absences), the poison control center, and so on. Individuals might say their telephone numbers for the others to dial.

- To reinforce letters of the alphabet, have learners look at the telephone and find which letters are not on the keypad (**Q** and **Z**).

- To reinforce letters and/or numbers, use correction fluid to delete several letters and/or numbers on a photocopy of the master. Then duplicate a copy for every learner. Have learners fill in the missing information.

Blackline Master 11: Clock

- Display a time on the clock. Ask a learner to say the time.

- Give each learner a copy of the Blackline Master. Help them cut out the hands and mount them with brads. Then say times and have learners display the time on their clocks. Check to make sure everyone has the correct time.

Blackline Master 12: Money

- Use the money to teach learners how to say amounts of money. Display various amounts and say how much you have, such as three hundred dollars. Have learners repeat.

- Set up a classroom store, supermarket, or mall. Have learners use the money to pay for purchases.

Blackline Master 13: Blank Check and Deposit Slip

- Use an overhead transparency of the master to model how to write and endorse checks and fill out deposit slips.

- Make multiple copies and have learners use them to "pay" various bills, such as utility bills, rent payments, and so on. You might bring in, or have learners bring in, real bills for them to look at and pay with checks.

- Bring in mail-order catalogs. Have the class imagine that they are going to buy an item. Help them make a selection, complete the order form, and pay with one of the checks.

- Have learners write checks to each other. Then have them endorse and complete deposit slips for their checks.

Competency Charts

The Individual Competency Charts on pages 150–154 allow teachers to record learners' success in acquiring *English ASAP*'s target recognition words and work skills. Spaces are provided to indicate the date of the assessment and to record the learners' success with a check mark. The Class Cumulative Competency Chart contains spaces to record learner names, work skills, and comments. You can record learner success with a check mark or the date of the assessment.

Certificate of Completion

The Certificate of Completion on page 156 allows you to recognize learners' successful mastery of all ten units of the book.

Start

➡️

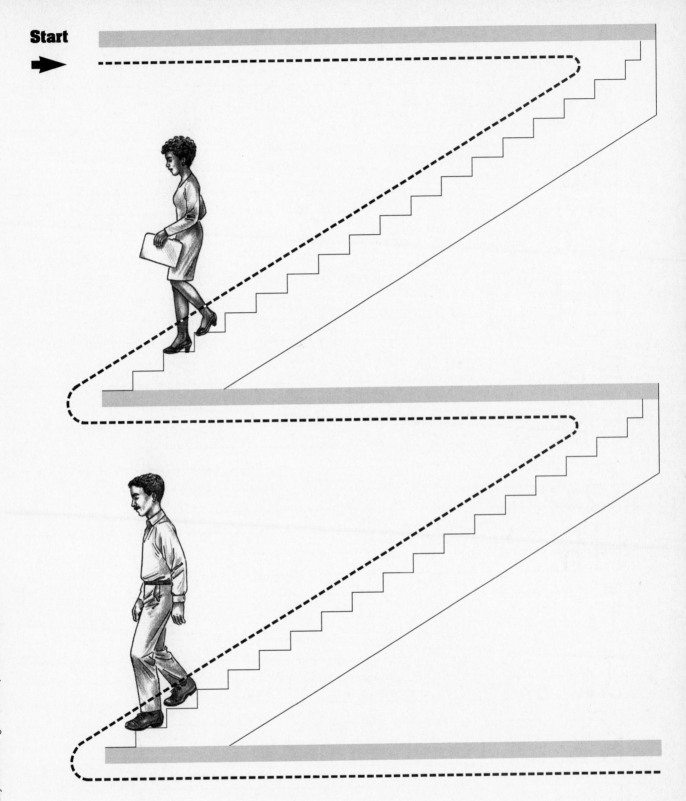

Blackline Master 1: Top-to Bottom and Left-to-Right Progression

A a

B b

C c

D d

E e

F f

G g

H h

I i

J j

K k

L l

M m

Blackline Master 2: Alphabet A–M

Nn

Oo

Pp

Qq

Rr

Ss

Tt

Uu

Vv

Ww

Xx

Yy

Zz

0
1
2
3
4
5
6
7
8
9
10
11
12
13

4
5
6
7
8
9
20
30
40
50
60
70
80
90

Blackline Master 5: Lined Paper

1. Listen.

2. Look.

3. Say.

4. Write.

Blackline Master 6: Common Directions

5. Circle.

6. Point.

7. Work with a partner.

8. Work with a team.

IDENTIFICATION FORM

Name	
Address	
City	State
Zip Code	Telephone Number

IDENTIFICATION FORM

NAME

ADDRESS

CITY   STATE   ZIP CODE

TELEPHONE NUMBER

THE STAR COMPANY

APPLICATION FOR EMPLOYMENT

Name:

Social Security Number:	Telephone Number:

Address:
_____
_____

Position applied for:	Date you can start:

Salary expected:

_____ an hour _____ a month _____ a year

☐ Full time

☐ Part time—If part time, hours you can work:

Monday–Friday: _____ Saturday/Sunday: _____

List any friends and/or relatives working with us now:

_____

_____

Are you over 21?   Yes ☐   No ☐

IMPORTANT TELEPHONE NUMBERS

Police	**911**
Fire Department	**911**
Ambulance	**911**

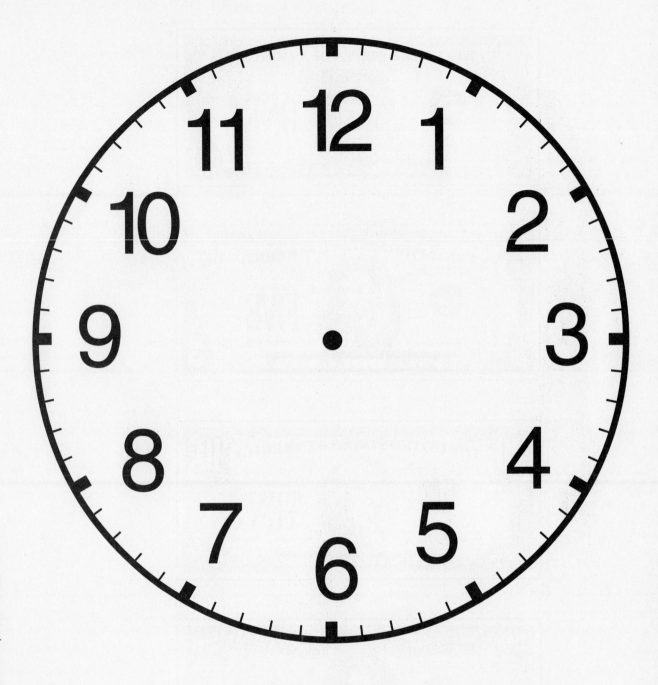

Blackline Master 11: Clock

147

Blackline Master 12: Money

550

_____

_____

_____   _____

PAY TO THE
ORDER OF _____ $ [   ]

_____ DOLLARS

✶**CITY**BANK

_____   _____

MEMO

DEPOSIT TICKET

Name _____

Address _____

_____

Date _____

_____

SIGN HERE

✶**CITY**BANK

CASH	
CHECKS	
TOTAL	

550

_____

_____

_____   _____

PAY TO THE
ORDER OF _____ $ [   ]

_____ DOLLARS

✶**CITY**BANK

_____   _____

MEMO

Individual Competency Chart

Learner _____

Class _____

Teacher _____

Unit 1

	Date Checked	Result (✔)	Comments
Work Skills			
Recognition Words			

Unit 2

	Date Checked	Result (✔)	Comments
Work Skills			
Recognition Words			

English ASAP

Individual Competency Chart

Learner _____

Class _____

Teacher _____

Unit 3

	Date Checked	Result (✔)	Comments
Work Skills			
Recognition Words			

Unit 4

	Date Checked	Result (✔)	Comments
Work Skills			
Recognition Words			

Individual Competency Chart

Learner _____

Class _____

Teacher _____

Unit 5

	Date Checked	Result (✔)	Comments
Work Skills			
Recognition Words			

Unit 6

	Date Checked	Result (✔)	Comments
Work Skills			
Recognition Words			

Individual Competency Chart

Learner _____

Class _____

Teacher _____

Unit 7

	Date Checked	Result (✔)	Comments
Work Skills			
Recognition Words			

Unit 8

	Date Checked	Result (✔)	Comments
Work Skills			
Recognition Words			

Individual Competency Chart

Learner _____

Class _____

Teacher _____

Unit 9

	Date Checked	Result (✔)	Comments
Work Skills			
Recognition Words			

Unit 10

	Date Checked	Result (✔)	Comments
Work Skills			
Recognition Words			

Class Cumulative Competency Chart

Unit _____   Class _____

Teacher _____

Work Skills

Name									Comments

English ASAP:

Connecting English to the Workplace

Certificate of Completion

This is to certify that

_____

has successfully completed the Literacy Level
of Steck-Vaughn's English ASAP series

Instructor _____

Organization or Program _____

City and State _____ Date _____

STECK-VAUGHN®
C O M P A N Y
A Division of Harcourt Brace & Company